Mediterranean

from HOMER to PICASSO

"For those born near the Mediterranean, there can be no doubt: Beauty does exist.

And how crazy to live far from it! How crazy and absurd to become exiled from it!

This is the Beauty of the fountain of Nîmes, the merest of fig trees, the tiniest vineyard tool shed,

at times not far from a pine—in some cases an umbrella pine.

It's the sparkling sea, fragments of a mosaic set among olive trees."

Francis Ponge, *Pour un Malherbe*

© 2001 Assouline Publishing, Inc. for the present edition
First published by Editions Assouline, Paris, France

Assouline Publishing, Inc.
601 West 26th Street
18th floor
New York, NY 10001
USA

www.assouline.com

Translated by Simon Pleasance & Fronza Woods

ISBN: 2 84323 245 7

Printed in Italy

XAVIER GIRARD

Mediterranean
from HOMER *to* PICASSO

ASSOULINE

Contents

For Jean-Yves Ravoux

Prologue

Its blue is like a chunk of that woad paste that used to be called a "paddy," or, in French, *cocagne*—a large, unevenly round ball suggesting a soft sky, before the advent of that somber and "sublime indigo." It's no good looking any further. The reasons for this book are right there in those lands, those *pays de cocagnes*, as the French call them, with their vivid blue violence and their ultramarine gentleness, between those silvery green olive trees and those orange-red roofs that make me think so vividly of a Fauve painting. They also lie in this imaginary land that has been given this name because the woad paddy used to be that poor wealth hidden in the blue.

I don't know if I am Mediterranean, but what I do know is that I come from these shores, the way people come from a mountain or a river. I am of these hills, these colors, these perfumes and this particular coast, which some bucolic bureaucrat inanely labeled "azure," as if it was not lapped by the sea. But maybe he was right after all. For a long time I didn't think it was a sea, but a bay or a lake. Summer after summer, when I headed towards the cliffs of the English Channel, between Dieppe and Le Tréport, I was eager to get back to "the real sea": a thick sea with storms whisking your feet off the ground, fishing shacks and real fishermen in yellow oilskins, like those mariners who Jean Ango dispatched across all the world's seas, huge cargo vessels in the distance plying through any kind of weather; a deep sea with tides you could hear a long way off, plashing with the cries of gulls; a sea that was more green and chalk than blatantly blue, reeking of iodine, which we inhaled like corpse-devouring ghouls. A sea that made our cheeks sting for two whole months, by dint of bestriding it day and night like real Fisher Kings.

Yet when it was time to head back south, I had "twinges of happiness" or "pangs of pleasure," as the Portuguese put it. I would rediscover the coves of Cape Ferrat, octopuses and sea urchins, spear fishing until nightfall, sweltering pine woods sheltering boulders, aloes, the beach at Passable, and diving off the Cap de Nice, to stop the summer from ending. The journey started before daybreak. We would take the Paris road, then after a stop in Versailles, it was the Nationale 7 through Charles Trenet and Jacques Tati's France, the France that *Pierrot le Fou* would soon be crossing straight to the sea, and the France that the spectacular accident in Godard's *Week-end* would usher into the contemporary era. The ritual was repeated year in, year out, necessary and delicious, like the picnic beside a canal or a river busy with dragonflies. Then we would cross to the other side of the Rubicon and be in the Mediterranean. The sea was still a long way off, but we were already there, because one of us had seen an olive tree. By the time we got to Valence, there was no doubt—those endless apricot trees,

Young Man, 5th century BCE.
For all those who have tried to describe the Mediterranean, it has the face of Antiquity. Statues are not just gods turned into artworks; they proceed ahead of us, and they have eyes to see with.

those tall cypresses staving off the fierce Mistral, those miles of peach trees sagging under the weight of their fruit, the muggy heat bearing down on us, all that tiredness, all of a sudden, crates of figs and heaps of melons spilling onto the roadside and hitting our faces with the sickly fragrance of overly long summers—this really was the Midi. At this point in the journey, we still had to wait a while before reaching our promised land, "dripping with milk and honey." We had to pass Aix, the Maures, the Estérel, endless Mandelieu and Antibes. At last, we arrived. The garden had the brownish-yellow hue of drought. Everything was baked by the sun. Straightaway I would yearn for those huge spring tides exposing the foreshore, up there in the west. The ritual of departure and homecoming could start all over again.

I realize, as I write, that my love for the landscape I was born in has been just a series of homecomings and journeys to the uttermost ends of the world. It's there, perhaps, that I came upon this idea that the Mediterranean— as it has also been for those exiled from it—is first and foremost an idealized dreamscape, a sentimental geography, whose real strength comes from the fact that we are not always in it, and thus imagine it all the more strongly. I remember the school term beginning, maybe in 1962, in a school built looking out over the sea, which the 1970s would do away with. Algerian Pieds-Noirs burst into my holiday world with a completely different vision of "my" sea. By forever leaving Pointe Pescade, Sidi Ferrouch and Mostaganem, they had left "another Mediterranean," as Jacques Berque calls it. *Paris Match* photos and radio newscasts had taught me that there was a Mediterranean at war on the far side. The books of Albert Camus and Audisio described for me a world that had the same tastes, the same flavor of sea urchins and *agua limone*, but for my school buddies, things weren't at all the same. On the other side it was another sea, another world. Over there, there was no "fair Midi." The sea of moderation and harmony of Hellenistic civilization, the Roman's *Mare Nostrum*, the shimmering bay of my days in those coves, all were just a "glorified cesspit," to use the words of Jean Sénac—just an image tattered and torn.

"The Mediterranean," wrote Bernard Pingaud in the pages of *L'Arc* in 1959, "is nothing other than the image we make of it for ourselves. The unusual thing is that we all make an image of it for ourselves, and that it is still a magnet for all those who are lucky enough to discover it one day. Herein lies a secret. It is perhaps not the secret conjured up by the 'land where the orange tree blooms.' It is the secret of this image itself, the secret of a dream which paradoxically contrasts abundance and drought, merriness and poverty, moderation and excess, joy and tragedy. Who can say why we need the Midi? If the Mediterranean didn't exist, we would have to invent it."

The purpose of this book is to question this secret contained in the images that we make for ourselves of the Mediterranean. It is not our intent to draw up a comprehensive overview of depictions of this sort of magnetic field that it defines for each one of us. Rather, with the help of some of its archetypes hailing both from the remote past and this modern day and age, we would invite readers to scan this vague boundary where images and reality merge and clash. As a huge projector of dreams and discourse, the Mediterranean cannot escape from portrayals of itself. Its truth resides less in a description of its geography and its historical structures than in the bedazzlement of its legends and the ongoing brilliance of its myths.

8

Blue sponged relief, 1958, Yves Klein.
"Y.K. Blue," which is so saturated in the artist's Mediterranean sensations, is a "dimensionless" blue, a blue that, in Yves Klein's own words, "makes the blood of sensibility flow." The blue-soaked sponges are a metaphor for our breathing.

HMATISSE 52

cohorts of Amphritrites and Venuses spreads across the strand. But do they really represent the Mediterranean? Nothing could be less certain.

The example of Puvis de Chavannes, who was one of the last allegorical painters, nowadays forsaken, is especially interesting. Between 1862 and 1867, at the request of architect Henri Espérandieu, when he produced the settings for the main staircase at Longchamp Palace, in Marseilles, the elected theme was the pagan city and the Christian city. The life of Pierre Puget, the city's Baroque painter and sculptor, should have acted as a thread. Puvis de Chavannes decided otherwise. Instead of the pagan city, he created a *Marseilles, Greek Colony*, which, as in the *Doux Pays*, one of his most famous compositions, featured Antiquity-like groups on a shore. Instead of the Christian city, Puvis came up with *Marseilles, Gateway to the Orient*. After initially planning to depict Marseilles harbor from the quays, like Vernet in his series of French ports, and many painters before him, he eventually decided to paint the city as seen from the sea. Here is his description: "Seen from the sea, the city is unfurled on the horizon. Its wharves invite the vessels heading for it. One of them, cut in half by the frame, forms a foreground, the ship's deck. We find every conceivable type, representing the different ethnic groups of the Levant: an Armenian, a Jew, a Greek, and an Arab naturally find their place and, mingling with sailors busying about their tasks, either seated or leaning on railings, they gaze at the sea of the Gauls. It's *Marseilles, Gateway to the Orient*."

The painting you see as you climb the museum steps is a rather frigid blue, barely warmed by the thick edging of fruit and flowers, painted, as Puvis indicated, in "natural hues": red and green peppers, prickly pears, banana leaves and bananas, decorative palms, begonias and watermelons. The new angle helped to dodge the port-painting genre, for which Puvis felt little gift, and it also had the advantage of setting up a more immediate link with the seaside scene of the second panel, where the sea was the main feature. But it still didn't become the decorative subject. Between the "sea of the Gauls" and the Orient, there was no room for the Mediterranean. The sea view, furthermore, lent the city a new breadth, something dazzling and vast, which Cézanne would remember from the Estaque. Puvis had never set foot in Marseilles, drawing his inspiration from photographs, so had he realized that there was something there other than a mere view— the emblem of a city? Jean-Claude Izzo likewise thought that it was impossible to understand Marseilles unless you broached it from the sea: "All you need do is arrive by ferry from Corsica," he wrote, "to connect with [its] history. Or, even simpler, return from a night fishing trip off the Estaque. When the roads open their arms to you, then, and only then, do you discover the eternal meaning of this city."

Aristide Maillol's work known by the title *Méditerranée*, which can be seen not only in Paris in the Tuileries gardens, but also in Perpignan, in the courtyard of the city hall, and on the sculptor's tomb in Banyuls, was first of all a "masterpiece" of pure sculpture. "In the spring of 1900," wrote Judith Cladel, "he took back to Paris a first cast of what he quite simply called *Woman Squatting* ..., he would model and mould it, rework the plaster, and five years' hard work then produced *Female Nude*, now famous as

Méditerranée." Throughout this period, the sculpture took on the massiveness and denseness "squared," which earned it the status of a manifesto of "primitive" classicism, stripped of the languor of 1900s statuary—a measured but stout work, monumental but sensual, classical but primitive. A sufficiently unusual—contemporaries identified Clotilde Narcisse, the sculptor's model and wife—and generalized representation to suit those advocating a forceful renewal of French classicism.

The plaster cast of *Woman Squatting,* which was shown at the 1905 autumn Salon, stirred Gide's enthusiasm: "She is beautiful, she doesn't mean anything; it's a silent work. I think we have to go way back to find such a complete neglect of all concerns unrelated to the mere illustration of beauty." It also fired Maurice Denis, who saw in it "a noble figure, at once expressive and harmonious, simple and great like the old days," a "systemless" work, unlike Matisse's painting, which the painter then spoke out against. The collector and patron Harry Kessler, an admirer of Maillol, ordered a stone version of the sculpture, which the sculptor would call *Statue for a Quiet Park,* and his client *Statue for a Shady Park.*

The work's semantic journey would undergo other twists and turns. During the 1920s, the sculpture commissioned by the government from Maillol appeared under the title of *Thought* and *Latin Thought,* "a term," Maillol explained to Judith Cladel, "to be taken in the sense that Charles Maurras gives it." The importance had caught up with the masterpiece to "silent" beauty that had made Gide marvel. Henceforth it would embody the Latin ideal of reconciliation between "the deities of pleasure" and the "intelligence, moderating, measuring or driving all the passions" that Maurras was theorizing about in those same years in his writings, the repercussions of which it is hard to imagine nowadays. "Does she not embody", wrote Judith Cladel, paraphrasing Maurras, "the land of light, the region of radiant intelligence, the Graeco-Roman zone where she took birth and the ancient breed of men peopling the edges?" Was the definitive title given it in the 1930s—*Méditerranée*—deemed less compromising than Latin Thought? Or in those years ushering in the return of the Greco-Latin order, wasn't the Mediterranean just another term for describing Latinness? In any event, the series of titles suggests that Maillol assumed the gradual shift to allegory of his *Female Nude* as an obvious fact of the period. Hadn't he after all titled one of his large 1895 paintings—a young woman by the sea who called Gauguin to mind—*La Côte d'Azur* or *La Méditerranée?*

Maurice Denis's *Méditerranée* similarly defines a territory common to the "primitive" and the "classical." In order to invent—in an often quite systematic way—this new Hellas, a mixture of the Atlantic island of Noirmoutier and the Esterel, the painter undertook to give the Breton coast the colors of the Mediterranean, by mixing, beneath a brilliant sky, the episodes of the Homeric narrative with beach games and seaside chats. Dionysos and his mounted attendants make their way amidst the bathers. Acis and Galatea enjoy the pleasures of boating. On the beach at Perros, Bacchus and Ariadne rub shoulders with mothers and children and turn-of-the-century bathing suits. Maurice Denis's message is clear: it is a matter, in a real allegory, of aligning the "everlasting summer" of the ancient Mediterranean and the "intimate

19

music" of contemporary France, the splendor of the bodies of Greek heroes and the pursuit of happiness on holiday beaches. What Gauguin set off in search of in the Marquesas Islands, Maurice Denis merely had to adapt, again and again, to the shores of the village of Le Pouldu, on the coast of Brittany. The Mediterranean myth converted to family values here illustrates, as the painter solemnly shows, "the realm of God and His justice," which was to be imposed on Catholic France, for which the painter campaigned.

Pierre Bonnard's works, which blend mythological beings with vacationers, as in the *The Abduction of Europa*, have their sights set elsewhere. Unlike Maurice Denis, Bonnard does not seek to make moral pronouncements about the pagan myth, but rather to disperse it in the seething spectacle of the Mediterranean shores. The sea that the painter discovered in the 1890s owes nothing to Maurras. In 1909, while staying with friends in St. Tropez, he wrote to his mother thus: "I have been smitten by the *Thousand and One Nights*, the sea, the yellow walls, the reflections that are as colorful as lights." Far from acting as a pretext for the introduction of new balance between pagan and Christian civilization, Midi beaches and Breton shores, for Bonnard the Mediterranean hastened the advent of an allegorical painting based on a profusion of highly colorful sensations. The "vision of a young girl, a shade darker than brown, in a pink shirt hanging down to her feet, proffering a huge blue macaw, at liberty, against a yellow, red and green background" made it obligatory to paint this folly as an outdoor representation.

It was a commission that prompted Bonnard to produce two works under the title *Méditerranée*: a triptych for the Russian collector Morosoff in 1911, a free-flowing evocation of a terraced garden above the sea, sheltered by the foliage of lush vegetation, and a series of four panels commissioned by the Bernheim family in 1916, which he completed in 1920. The composition consists of two pastoral scenes: a modern scene, *Workers at the Grande Jatte*, and an allegory of the Mediterranean, *La Méditerranée* or *Les Monuments*. This latter painting adopted the viewpoint that Puvis had dropped: the harbor at St. Tropez, which Bonnard had already depicted, seen from the quay. The quotation of Claude Gellée's (known as Le Lorrain) imaginary ports probably acted as a guide. Bonnard distributed the setting for his "monuments" on either side of a perspective quickened by emphasizing the contrivedness of the scenery, adding contrasting plans and phony links at will. His *Méditerranée* is a deliciously flawed construction, an assemblage that in no way masks its tricks. But it is also a space of improbabilities and fairylike confusions. Figures walking to the fountain loom from the bas-reliefs. The statue of Cleopatra in the foreground, which may call De Chirico to mind, seems to be stirring from its petrified dream. The boundary between the imaginary monuments and St. Tropez harbor is vague. The whole panel seems contained within the drawing of an eye that is having trouble dealing with what it sees. Bonnard's *La Méditerranée* is first and foremost the experience of this wonderful indecisiveness. The fairylike quality of the landscape here is so striking that it doesn't permit any distinction between what belongs to the visible world and what belongs to the creations of memory.

21

Méditerranée, 1905, Aristide Maillol.
"She was eventually called Mediterranean..." (Judith Cladel)

The Joy of Life,
1905–1906,
Henri Matisse.
The Joy of Life *is*
one of the most
flamboyant
allegories of the
Mediterranean in
Matisse's oeuvre.
The picture borrows
from ancient
literature and
iconography as
much as from
Mallarmé, and from
Ingres as much as
from Cézanne, and
would even draw
from prehistory.
It freezes a vision
dedicated to the
belief in happiness
conceived as
"the harmonious
satisfaction of many
different desires."
(Paul Diel)

But it is *Le Voyage*, another decorative panel painted between 1906 and 1910 for Misia Natanson, that comes closest to an allegory of the Mediterranean. Surrounded by an "African" border peopled by monkeys and parrots, the Mediterranean of *Le Voyage* is an indigo lake with naiads and dolphins frolicking in front of a schooner. The sea is hemmed by an oriental city and shows an island inhabited by a mandarin. This decorative fantasy with its muted hues actually owes very little to the real Mediterranean, which the painter turned to at the same time and which would emerge, mingled with memories of Normandy, in the vast pastoral works to come.

We find no *Méditerranée* in Matisse's corpus, but a good many of his works have the Mediterranean myth as their implicit subject. One of them reminds us that the painter one day took part in the casting of the *Méditerranée* in Maillol's studio. This is the series of cut-out gouaches titled *Blue Nude* (1954), whose success with the public possibly had to do with the fact the people recognized in it an allegorical representation of the sea. The sculptural power of the cut-out form and the blue color form the figure which is in perfect synthesis with the Inland Sea, as classical culture and modernity, in its heyday, conceived it. For Matisse, the Mediterranean was not a set but the best possible kind of pictorial material, the colored substance you could get into "without any contradiction," as in *The Wave*, produced in the same period. The *Blue Nude* is actually presented to us like a celestial Venus—the Venus *coelestis* of Plato's *Banquet*— as opposed to the Venus *naturalis* of the tradition of female nudes extending from Titian to Picasso. But it is also the Mediterranean Venus in all her sculptural glory.

From *Luxe, calme et volupté* (1904) and *The Joy of Life* (1905) to *The Dance* (1930–33), commissioned by the Barnes Foundation, the allegory of the sea merges in Matisse's work with the evocation of an original Mediterranean, prior to the forms of classicism. If the figures in *Luxe, calme et volupté* still seem bent on combining the contemporary scene and models hailing from the school in a pointillist *Doux pays*, *The Joy of Life* would go straight to prehistory for the sources of a Mediterranean golden age. *Luxe I* and *II* (1907), and the subsequent works filled with gigantic figures, give this vision of the Mediterranean the allegorical dimension of a land haunted by the gods.

Picasso produced just a small canvas called *Méditerranée*, which he featured in *Le Tub* (1901) in the Phillips Collection. The Mediterranean theme would spill out of the neoclassical period to which it is ordinarily linked. *Pipes of Pan* (1923), which springs to mind first, is just one of the more famous versions of a Mediterranean cult, with countless examples. In it, Picasso stages an ancient pastoral: two adolescents pose by the sea, rendered salient by the cubic lines of a setting reduced to its bare essentials. This picture, on view in the Picasso Museum in Paris, acts like an enigma. The public isn't taken in, as it stops to look silently at this most meditative of scenes. The amorous serenade, which a recent x-ray study has brought to light, reveals that the point of departure of this picture was a variation on a Pompeian theme—recalling Picasso's visit to Pompeii in 1917, with Diaghilev, Cocteau and Massine. The Pompeian fantasy that

24

Bacchus and Ariadne, 1907, Maurice Denis (detail).
The mythological Mediterranean of Titian and Poussin transplanted to the Breton beach of Trestrignel, at Perros, with the Seven Isles on the horizon; peplum and striped bathrobe; the risky combination of the love between Thesus and Ariadne and middle-class holidays in France in 1907.

inspired it was mixed—according to Anne Baldessari—with the photographic documentation of the visit showing Picasso and Massine posing in front of a fountain, and a picture of the gardens of Marcus Lucretius. The two young people imitate the position of Mars and Venus, the way Picasso imitated Bacchus' posture in another photo. This ancient role-playing was one of the sources of the work, and explains the changes occurring during its execution. Picasso no longer represents the frescoes themselves, but the replica that the dancer and the painter had improvised for the photograph. Picasso's Mediterranean is altogether complete here: in it, antiquity is less important than the mimics. His figures are less models than interactive images. Illuminated by the same dense light that turns them into statues in the photograph, the two adolescent boys are posing for eternity. So it was in Antibes that Picasso pictured the Mediterranean.

Farewell to Crete (1984), by Malcolm Morley, is a mix of Cretan landscape and Long Island beach. It is also a recollection of a journey made by the painter two years before to Crete and Greece. A Trojan horse and a priapic figure loom up on a crowded beach. Morley explains the story behind the picture thus: "There was this head in a museum in Crete, in a display case, and in another the body of a man holding a fishing net, just as if he were holding a phallus. I put them together, but I unintentionally left a gap between the head and the body. Then I started to transfer it on to a grid, and as I painted I realized that I'd moved a line up. I left it like that. I didn't imagine that the gap would go right through the eyes. It produced a very interesting result." Like *Pipes of Pan*, Morley's picture proceeds by association and abrupt sundering, shifting to another line and another intensity. The Trojan horse on the Long Island beach calls to mind Dionysos' chariot on Maurice Denis's Breton beach. But Morley is actually closer to Bonnard. His Trojan horse is an accessory, a tourist souvenir, and the age-old Mediterranean which he depicts is a rough-hewn montage that displays its phony links and its comical discrepancies, in order to underscore its allegorical character.

Pipes of Pan, 1923, Pablo Picasso.
Palimpsest Mediterranean: beneath the standing young man, x-rays have revealed an embracing couple with a cupid above them; behind these two Castor and Pollux-like figures lurk Picasso and Leonid Massine at Pompeii, in the garden of Marcus Lucretius, as well as Mars and Venus, and even a hermaphroditic Bacchus and Cupid: beneath the classical pastoral, the amorous serenade of two adolescents.

[Pages 28–29] *La Femme au chien*, 1924–1926, Francis Picabia.
The "flashy" Venus with a Pinocchio-like nose: an allegory of an anti-Côte d'Azur, when the Mediterranean of vacationers belies Homer's "enchanted shores."

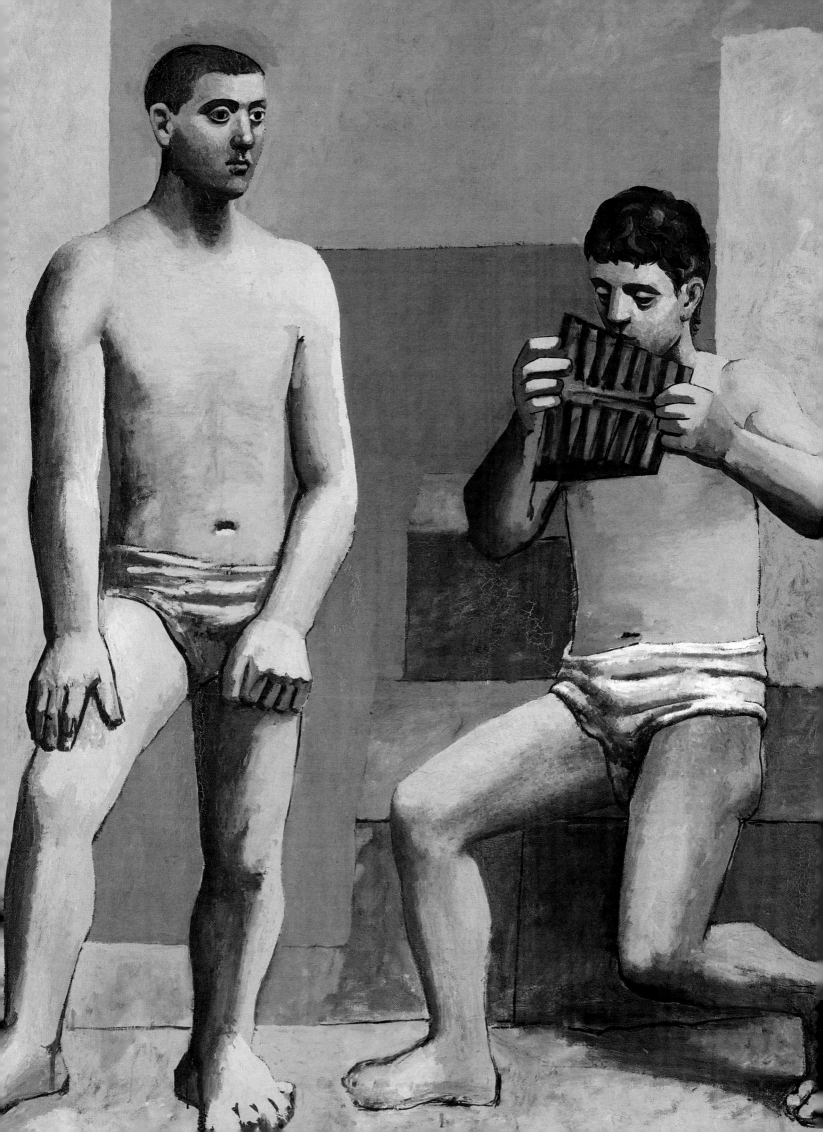

he brought back had a ghostlike tone about them, emphasized by the technique of the calotype (an early photographic negative process), which the presence of the guide was possibly designed to temper.

Throughout the 1850s and 1860s, plenty of photographic teams flocked to Egypt: Teynard in 1851, Salzmann in 1854, Greene in 1855, de Clerq in 1859. Little by little, reporting from Egypt shed its scientific pretext, and turned its gaze on contemporary Egypt (Teynard), and broadened its area of investigation to the Christian Orient (Salzmann). Hector Horeau's *Sites les plus célèbres et les plus intéressants de l'Egypte et de la Nubie*, in 1840–1842, and the human types photographed in 1855 by Auguste Bartholdi and then by Félix Teynard in 1858, all helped to popularize the image of the Orient that had been put to one side by the monumental vision of the earlier researchers. Henceforth, the photographer worked for the traveller.

"Heliographic teams" traveled to the South of France to document the monuments of the Romanesque and medieval Mediterranean, such as Baldus in Avignon and Carcassonne. Others, like Gustave Le Gray in about 1856–59, went to the Mediterranean, following the example of painters, to produce the first photographic *Marines* or seascapes. The famous *Great Wave at Sète* and the *Broken Wave* was the first of a genre seeking to be instantaneous: "Seascapes under sail and on the move, a rough sea, clouds floating in the air, the sun itself with its broad majestic rays, are reproduced and set down instantly and simultaneously, without any sleight of hand and without any tricks," Le Gray proudly wrote, omitting to specify that for the *Great Wave at Sète* he had access to two negatives, one for the sky, the other for the sea, so as to produce the desired light effect. Courbet, who had inspired what Le Gray was looking for, drew inspiration from him in turn. But the present-day interest in Le Gray's seascapes—leaving their historical interest aside—lies more in their minimalism than in the secret behind their making.

For the very first time, huge expanses were photographed for their own sake, with no monument involved other than their glowing vastness. But it was in the photo collections of regional studios, becoming more and more numerous in these same years, that the Mediterranean started to appear. Each great metropolis had its own: in Italy, for example, Giorgio Sommer opened a studio in Naples, the Alinari brothers did the same in Florence, Carlo Naya in Venice and Vicenzo Galdi in Rome. Visions of cities under construction, scenes of jubilation, minor crafts and trades, morning streets, disasters and gatherings: the photograph chronicled the Mediterranean world day in and day out, in the hubbub of beloved places and memorable events.

Nowadays, books bring together and compile these pictures of bygone days with a pungent whiff of nostalgia. With its tide of imagery, the tourist album has meanwhile overwhelmed the contemplative wonder of these pictures. In so doing, it forced the eye to stock up on views, so as to put together a repertory of themes that are so present that our reflex, in discovering certain sites, will be to recognize in them the illusion and sham of the representation we have made of them. "My God," exclaimed Duane Michaels at Karnak, "it looks like one Cecil B. DeMille's early movies!"

46

Fred on his Ladder at the Parthenon, Greece, 1907, self-portrait of Frédéric Boissonas.
Boissonnas at the top of his ladder, or the viewpoint of Lord Elgin, who, in 1802,
stocked up with "mutilated artistic blocks," as Byron observed.

[Pages 48–49] View of the Acropolis at Sounion, Attica, Cape Sounion, George Hoyningen-Huene.
"It deserves to be glorified..." (Elytis)

The adventure of Victor Bérard and Frédéric Boissonnas, the famous Swiss photographer, offers a perfect example of this preeminence of representations over the photographed landscape. Armed with his Téléphot, Frédéric Boissonnas started to take photos for Victor Bérard in 1903, at Ithaca. Boissonnas still found Greece intact and, more importantly, less photographed than Egypt: "There's a whole world to be discovered," he wrote, "and scenery and landscapes to be recorded." From a second journey undertaken in 1907, he brought back a series of photographs of monuments which had never before been seen at such close quarters, or lit with such painstaking care, light years away from back-to-Egypt ghostly landscapes. The following year saw another journey embarked upon with the writer Daniel Baud-Bovy, with whom he would produce a luxurious album. "In those places where others went merely to look for ruins," the latter wrote, "we discovered a nature and a people."

Charles-Albert Cingria sang the praises of their report in which it was possible to see "Greek soldiers in their *fustanellas* skirts, side by side in the same orderly scenery with those old-fashioned and voluminous outer garments called *Pallae*, Turkish shops with *Taygete*-like figures for botanists." Contemporary Greece had joined up with ancient Hellas to establish the poem's reality. When in Ceuta in 1912 with Bérard, looking for the Calypso cave, the photographer recounted: "We climbed. The site was quite lovely. Bérard dashed through the bushes. I heard him shriek. Heavens! Had he fallen into the hands of the Berbers ...? No! He reemerged waving his hat, hopping up and down, doing a Pyrrhic dance. Boissonnas! Boissonnas! The cave! Homer's four springs! Come and see, they're running. Four, four I tell you... It's all there, incredible. Bérard declaimed the landscapes of Homer. He was exultant, triumphant. He thought of all the criticisms and mockery endured for the past ten years... Ah! the cretins! We'll give 'em something that'll go with your photo, Boissonnas..." To authenticate the find, once and for all, the photographer took a photo of "the climbing vine and clumps of parsley described by the Homeric text." That same year, with Louis Bertrand, Boissonnas followed in the footsteps of St. Augustine to recreate the Latin Africa dear to the author of *The Blood of the Races*. On another occasion, in his frantic quest for the geographical truth of the ancient writings, Boissonnas went rushing off on the trail of the Bible. Whether it be a matter of drawing up an inventory of Egyptian monuments or the sites of *The Odyssey*, photographic reporting is reliant upon an archaeological conception of the Mediterranean.

When Herbert List went to Greece in 1937, accompanied by George Hoyningen-Huene, he was seeking a metaphysical landscape. Associating with the Surrealists, plus the example of De Chirico and Max Ernst, led the photographer to set up an enigmatic little theatre in the most desolate parts of the Lukabittos mountains, north east of the Acropolis. Many of List's photographs are filled with monumental objects, shrouded in their mystery, placed in the stage set of the image and illuminated by theatrical lighting. The collection of photographs planned in 1937–1938 was to be called *Licht über Hellas* or *Light over Hellas*. The work would be prefaced with an introduction by Hugo von Hofmannsthal describing the light of

50

View of the Villa Malaparte, 1998, Karl Lagerfeld.
The villa on Cape Massullo, on Capri—which is not so much a manifesto for rationalist architecture, but rather a Mediterranean mausoleum, a "portrait in stone" of the writer, a "house like me," as Malaparte himself wrote, built in a place "appropriate solely for strong men and free spirits"—was the work of Adalberto Libera (EUR architect in Rome) and Curzio Malaparte. Godard used it for one of his sets in his film Contempt.

Greece, which is "inexpressibly harsh and inexpressibly soft all at once ... highlighting the tiniest detail with a gentle clarity ... that makes our hearts beat faster." Among the loveliest pictures of List's Greek sojourn, the glass standing in the light and the bottles of a still life set up, casually on a table by the sea are like luminous offerings. Other photographs only seem to see in ancient monuments an interplay of perfect volumes in the light. In the clarity enveloping them, the scattered fishermen and young people photographed also find a nobility that links them with their remote models. List looked on Greece as the country where beauty existed simply by way of the magic of light: an octopus drying, a chair on a shore, a bowl with a goldfish in front of a bay window in the setting sun, a glass of water, a boy in bathing trunks, a temple. All are equally interesting, and all just as hallowed by the splendor of the Greek sun. "It deserves to be glorified," (*Tu Axion Esti*) as Elytis wrote in his famous collection, holds good here, in the broad light.

52

Three thousand eight hundred kilometers from Gibraltar to Syria, seven hundred between Genoa and Tunisia, just a hundred and thirty-eight from Sicily to Cap Bon, three million square kilometers as opposed to the Pacific Ocean's sixty-eight... The Mediterranean: a sea in a bottle.

Representations

Films

The film guide announces the screening of a series of films devoted to the "Mediterranean crossroads." Beneath a picture of the harbor at Cassis, taken from Jonas Mekas' *Notes for Jérôme* (1966–1978), the title of the article is, needless to add, "Mother Mediterranean." The Mediterranean on film! The subject is scholarly—the author quotes Dominique Fernandez and Fernand Braudel—and pleasant, but is it really the subject? What part does the Mediterranean play in the films that are made every year on its shores? Is it just a set, or an essential theme? Geographical daydream or real space? Is just the Mediterranean involved? Or is it the whole Midi?

Which Mediterranean do Robert Guédiguian's films talk about, for example? Is *Marius and Jeannette* (1997) a Mediterranean film? Or is it rather a film in the tradition of between-the-wars southern cinema, as its title, paying tribute to Pagnol, suggests? The dialogue, characters and sets are all of the Midi. L'Estaque, the arbor cobbled together for eating aïoli, taking a siesta, drinking rosé wine, with the windows opening on to the street so you can stick your head outside to have a chat, football, and summer nights too. The story—"Happiness regained by two beings who have been greatly exercised by life" (Jean-Claude Loiseau, *Télérama*)—is a bit less so. The virtual absence of the sea—people hardly ever swim in it and when they do it's in a gingerly way, they hardly ever fish in it (fish arrive straight in the bistro tanks and end up on the floor at a fistfight) and they never even look at it—is, on the contrary, a hallmark of "Mediterranean-ness." The Mediterranean is possibly there where it's least expected, in what we might call the spirit of "shiftless loafing"—"Vitellonism," as it were—that underpins the film: the attachment of men to their women and their neighborhood, like the shiftless young "slackers" in Federico Fellini's *The Young and The Passionate*, incapable of leaving their mammas and Rimini, the famous beach.

A scene from Elia Kazan's *America America*—probably the greatest film ever devoted to the Inland Sea—sets forth what might well be the Mediterranean's snare of happiness. In his carpet shop in Istanbul, Stavros's future father-in-law describes to this candidate for exile the life that awaits him if he reneges on his plan: "We'll be here, Stavros, with women to look after us. And we'll wait, and the years will go by, winter here, summer on the island. You'll grow heavy, we'll watch the time pass, you'll grow older, I'll be old, we'll be sitting there, the two of us, you and me. We'll eat, we'll drink, we'll loosen our clothes and have a little siesta, side by side. We'll wake up, we'll have a game of backgammon and it'll be time for a glass of ouzo with olives and cheese."

The theme of the simple, unchanging life within a protected perimeter, while the world all around is tearing itself apart, is at the hub of Gabrielle Salvatores' *Mediterraneo* (1991). The film tells the tale of eight Italian

54

The horse-man and the poet in Jean Cocteau's *The Testament of Orpheus* (1960).
The Valley of Hell, September 1959; in the abstract maze of Les Baux-de-Provence, Cocteau-cum-Theseus filmed, life-size, a fantasy Antiquity that was more real than all the historical epics in film history.

soldiers in the Second World War, who are stranded on an island in the Aegean, where they rediscover the basic truths of group living beneath the Mediterranean sun.

Masterpieces—Jean-Luc Godard's *Contempt*, for example—that give a central role to the Mediterranean are actually quite rare. Godard's film, shot in Rome and on Capri in 1963, is also, in his own words, "the story of shipwrecks from the western world, of survivors of the shipwreck of modernity who one day, like heroes out of Verne and Stevenson, reach a mysterious desert island, whose mystery is inexorably the absence of mystery, in other words, truth." *Contempt* starts like Orson Welles' *The Magnificent Ambersons* and Jean Cocteau's *The Testament of Orpheus*, with the famous voice-over of the credits over the sunny images of a boulevard at Cinecittà, down which walks a small group of the film's characters: "It's based on Alberto Moravia's novel. There's Brigitte Bardot and Michel Piccoli. There's also Jack Palance and Giorgia Moll. And Fritz Lang," etc. The voice might be that of the Greek bard of the Homeric song which introduces the Athenian banquet by summoning the guests by their names. Borne along by Georges Delerue's symphonic music, the credits end with the ritual, erudite citation, while the camera films the film crew in action against the blue sky: "Film," said André Bazin, "replaces the way we see things with a world that is in tune with our desire. *Contempt* is the story of this world."

The title, in tall, bright red Roman characters, then spreads across the entire screen: dramatic red of the inscription, dazzling white of the walls, cobalt blue of the sky, glowing yellow of a fine spring day in Rome: the brilliant tonality of the film is set. It's the tonality of Matisse's cut-out gouaches and of 1960s design. It's also the color of a shadowless film, shot in broad daylight, head-on, cut into the flesh of pure colors which side with each other like characters: the producer's red Alfa Romeo, Paul and Camille's red and white towels, the yellow bathrobes, BB's black wig. To distinguish the sequences taken from Fritz Lang's *Odyssey* from the film's other scenes, Godard cranks up the chromatic intensity a notch or two: "The colors," he notes, "will be brighter, more

56

Contempt, Jean-Luc Godard, 1960.
"This, by the by, is what I like in general in the cinema, an overload of magnificent signs which bask in the light of their inexplicability." (Jean-Luc Godard)

contrasting, and harsher, in addition to the way they're organized [than those of the film itself]. Let's say that they'll have the effect of a Matisse or a Braque picture in the midst of a Fragonard composition or an Eisenstein shot in a Rouch movie." In reality, *Contempt* is the most luminous of films, from start to finish. Dominated "by the deep blue of the seas [*sic*], the red of the villa and the yellow of the sun," the film's second part is merely launched along a more abrupt Mediterranean line which plunges straight into *The Odyssey* and its chromatic world. Godard adds: "We'll also find a certain trichromatic printing, fairly close to real ancient statuary."

Jean-Daniel Pollet's *Méditerranée*, a short cult film on the theme of death and beauty in the Mediterranean region, was shot in the same year as *Contempt*. The Algerian war was just over. In this film, the Mediterranean is hemmed by barbed wire and abandoned bunkers, and filmed like a lake of memory crushed by "the impression of oldness," as we are told in a voice-over reading of Philippe Sollers' beautiful text. Two faces appear endlessly like the two faces of one and the same silent god: on one side, the face of death, obsessively depicted by a slumbering Eve on an operating table, a mummy with lips ajar, the golden mask of Tutankhamen, the bull slaughtered (not without difficulty) on the grey sand of a bullring; and, on the other, the face of beauty, depicted by the light, majestic landscapes, temples, the seaside party, a young girl buttoning her dress, and another girl arranging her hair. The film tirelessly questions these two aspects of the Mediterranean, endlessly returning to the killing of the bull and the abandoned Cleopatra, as if the enigma of Mediterranean civilization resided in a crime committed at the dawn of time and incessantly represented. Under its experimental exterior, the film is actually part and parcel of the Romantic tradition which—from Chateaubriand to Thomas Mann by way of Barrès—turns the Mediterranean into the original site of civilizations and the scene of their death throes.

The undoubted masterpiece in this tradition is Luchino Visconti's *Death in Venice* (1971). What Gustav Aschenbach desperately questions, in Tadzio's beauty (another silent god) is nothing other than the sealed promise of Greek statuary. "His face," wrote Thomas Mann of the young Tadzio, "pale and elegantly closed beneath honey-colored curly hair, the straight nose, the adorable mouth with its air of gentle and divine solemnity, called to mind the Greek statuary of the finest period and showed in the sheer perfection of its form a charm so unusual that Aschenbach thought he had never before set eyes on a more complete masterpiece, either in nature or in art." Like a "magnificent-haired young man removing a thorn," Hyakinthos, Endymion and Narcissus rolled into one, Tadzio is an inaccessible god who gazes back at Aschenbach. He is the god of the outer edges, as harbingered by the twilight of aristocratic Europe in 1914; he is the god of the sea, realm of the "inarticulate" and the "incomparable."

From the sea, Fellini calls forth the beauty of Rimini's female summer visitors, as well as the sea monster in *La Dolce Vita* and *Satyricon*. It's on the sea, in Naples, that he embarks the ailing—and malodorous—elephant in *And The Ship Sails On*, which the film's narrator saves from shipwreck. Fellini's Mediterranean is also a place

of childhood—in Rimini, where he was born, Fellini recalls "the summer in the great dazzling sun, half-naked bodies running towards the sea in a rowdy din of voices, music and the metallic voice of a loudspeaker repeating the name of a little girl whose parents have lost her." Here, too, washed up on the beach, there's a rotting sea creature. The Mediterranean is at once childhood and death, to an obsessive degree; it's the sea of see-through plastic where Gloria N. sets sail to scatter the ashes of the singer Edmée Tétua off the isle of Erimo, and the sea which depicts in miniature the Trevi fountain into which Anita Ekburg plunged.

Buñuel's films also deal with death, sea and putrefaction. The Spanish filmmaker, who was born in Aragon, saw the Mediterranean as the thoroughfare of the two greatest scourges of contemporary Spain: the Roman Empire and the Catholic church. It was on its shores, close to Dali's home at Cadaques, that he filmed, in *L'Age d'or*, the

Death in Venice, Luchino Visconti, 1970.
Hugo von Hofmannsthal in Greece:
"The eyes of the statues were
suddenly turned on me and an absolutely
indescribable smile played on their faces."

Monica Vitti in Sicily, in *L'Avventura*
by Michelangelo Antonioni, 1960.
The beauty of the Mediterranean, like that of the desert in Profession
Reporter *and* Zabriskie Point, *isn't there for anybody in particular,*
or, rather, it hews out, between the character and the world, an abyss
that nothing can fill in—not even the soaring, overhanging viewpoint.

memorable sequence of the inauguration ceremony bringing the people of Majorca together around the authorities; a ceremony with speeches interrupted by the appearance of the skeletons of the archbishops wearing their mitres and their ecclesiastical vestments, and by the couple lying in a muddy pond, in a fierce embrace which shocks the gathering. To wind up the scene, Buñuel brings in the sound of a lavatory flushing in as explicit a way as possible. The next sequence takes place in Rome, "age-old seat of the Church," in "the year of grace 1930," as the title specifies. The images of "imperial Rome" mix classical views of monuments, the Vatican, gates, fountains, statues, a bookshop and the contemporary street. The audience realizes that there is no help forthcoming here: the putrefaction of the Church, and of order, is like a dead donkey or a bishop's corpse. Tristana—played by Catherine Deneuve—leans over the alabaster effigy of Cardinal Tavera with the same attentiveness as Buñuel does over the exposed corpse of the ultraconservative archbishop of Saragossa, Soldevila Romero, who was assassinated by anarchists.

But putrefaction does not come solely from the sea. Buñuel asserts as much with a kind of scary sadism in the documentary titled *Land without Bread* (1933), which he made just after *L'Age d'or*. It is set in the heart of Extremadura, between Caceres and Salamanca, stuck in the wretched poverty of the Spanish peasantry of this farflung corner that calls to mind Carlo Levi's Lucania and its sequestered people.

In spite of less nightmarish exteriors, it is by no means certain that Michelangelo Antonioni's Mediterranean offers greater optimism than Buñuel's with its "recalcitrant cadavers." In *L'Avventura* (1959), the beauty of the Lipari islands and Sicily around Catania, Noto and Taormina points with every shot to the private disaster of the protagonists. The isle of idyllic holidays that we spy from the yacht is the trap in which Anna (Lea Massari) goes astray, and Sicily will finish off the love between Sandro and Claudia (Monica Viti). Antonioni often said that he needed a landscape to give substance to a story. The Mediterranean of *L'Avventura* is that of a sentimental odyssey that ends up in an extinct volcano. The outskirts of Ravenna which act as a backdrop in *Il Deserto rosso* (1964) are on a par with the fates of the threesome: husband, lover and wife. The chromatic intensity of the film, which likens it to the Pop Art and New Realism of those same years, further heightens the kind of fatal upset that, here too, unravels the bonds between the people, the way a red and blue poster is torn to shreds in a placeless no-man's-land.

"In this film," wrote Rossellini about *Voyage in Italy* (1953), "I tried to show the Mediterranean peoples, the Latin peoples, as they really are and not the way Anglo-Saxons and people from the North always see them, coming south as they do to look at us like animals in a zoo." The splendor of Naples, Villa Torre Del Greco, Pompeii, Herculanum and Capri, where the couple travel, also accompanies the end of love. But Rossellini grants it an almost mystical value which Antonioni never imagines: "Showing Italy," the director notes, "Naples, that strange atmosphere with its intermingling of a very real, very immediate, very profound feeling, the feeling of everlasting life; it's something that's completely vanished from the world."

Jean-Paul Belmondo and Anna Karina in *Pierrot le Fou*, Jean-Luc Godard, 1965.
Marianne [off-screen]: Did they find it?
Ferdinand: What?
Marianne: Eternity.
Ferdinand: It's the sea meeting.
Marianne: With the sun.
(Arthur Rimbaud/Jean-Luc Godard)

Ulysses

He's the hero who, like no other hero, embodies the Mediterranean, symbolizing as he does the universal traveller, emblazoned outside all the world's travel agencies. Yet all this "ever-wandering man" really wants is to go home. The wily mariner loathes the sea. All the valiant warrior thinks about is laying down his arms. And the warmhearted companion has thoughts only for revenge. Just like the opening words of Marcel Proust's *In Search of Lost Time*, we retain the beginning of Ulysses' adventures, and so the whole tale:

> *Tell me, Muse, the story of that resourceful man who was*
> *driven to wander far and wide after he had sacked the holy citadel of Troy.*
> *He saw the cities of many people and he learnt their ways.*
> *He suffered great anguish on the high seas...*

He is also the "well-advised," "the inventive man with a thousand ruses," "the man of a thousand tricks," "hard-working" and "refined," "skilled in every manner of game," and possessed by an obsession. As a skilled craftsman and brilliant storyteller, he has quick tricks up his sleeve and is no less quick-witted, but he also knows that his resourcefulness has a sister: hard times. "Beauty, reason, the gift of the gab: it is quite clear, he replies to Euryalus [who had treated him like some common charterer], staring at him with a baleful eye, the gods don't give us all our gifts at once."

Ulysses is not a god, he is simply crafty like the goddess Metis who, with Athena, reigned over the cunning intelligence of the Greeks. Like the Mediterranean fisherman who, to survive, turns occasionally into a guide, or a knickknack vendor, or someone renting out rooms, he practises the "art of diversity," overlooking no expedient or lure.

As a gentle carpenter and an experienced sailor, he can also be a formidable "plunderer of cities." To achieve his ends, he shows himself to be cautious to the point of slowness and as quick as a ferret. After mature reflection, he will choose not to choose. Naked, "all aglow with charm and beauty" before a perplexed Nausicaa, the hero waxes pensive:

> *[He] considered whether he should throw his arms round the beautiful girl's*
> *knees and beg for help, or just keep his distance and beg her*
> *with all courtesy to give him clothing and direct him to the city.*
> *He decided that as the lady might take offence if he embraced her knees,*
> *it would be better to keep his distance and courteously plead his case...*

A Roman mosaic depicting the head of Oceanus, in the *frigidarium* of the hot baths at Themetra, southwest of Sousse, Tunisia. *Oceanus does indeed have a head as huge as the "river Ocean." The Mediterranean, for its part, must wait to be seated at the banquet of the gods, to be no longer a "complex of seas" but a character in her own right.*

In front of an unbelieving Penelope, "Ulysses invented everything but passed it all off as true." In *The Iliad* he had already managed to use "winged words," so light that you'd have said that "they were falling like snowflakes in winter." In a word, "his mind was never short of a trick or two." His skills as a craftsman are as many and varied as the figures of speech in his conversation. His mind is like a multicolored fabric or a sparkling weapon: he knows both how to seduce and play at being a half-wit. "At times," wrote Pietro Citati in *The Light of the Night*, "he appears before us like a noble hero radiating elegance and beauty, wrapped in a thick purple cloak; and at times, quite to the contrary, like an old beggar with bleary eyes, his skin shriveled, clad in smoke-blackened tatters, carrying a repulsive bag. At times you'd think he was a lion, striding through wind and rain with eyes like glowing embers, and at times an octopus, with his slimy head and clinging tentacles, clutching a rock; sometimes he's a mighty eagle speaking in human tongues, and at times a cautious, ravenous vulture ... We don't know which face to choose, or which creature to prefer; and in the end, we seem to glimpse, in the varying light and mist of the Mediterranean, a kind of sea

griffon, with a lion's head and an octopus's tentacles, the wings of an eagle and the beak of a vulture."

Yet all these transformations have just one purpose: to find "Ithaca the clear," the bed of Penelope and her son Telemachus. Because his companions failed to "smell the trap," they were turned into swine or let themselves be put to sleep. Ulysses can indeed journey to the uttermost ends of the land of the "last men" (the Ethiopians), visit the realm of the dead and spend time with the gods, but he'll never be tempted to pass by on the other side. The idea of becoming a "dolphin man" like Jacques Mayol in Luc Besson's *The Big Blue* doesn't occur to him one single time. His arena is that of the "bread-eaters," the "wheat-bearing land," meals of bread and grilled meat washed down with "dark wine" diluted with water, to the accompaniment of the bard, and not that of the fruit-and-flower-eating Lotus-eaters, the Lestrygons and the fearsome man-eating Cyclopes. His ideal is that of a simple man, reproached for being too down-to-earth. At the end of *The Republic*, Plato shows Ulysses opting for "the

Ulysses and Polyphemus, color print after L. du Bois-Reymond, circa 1910.
In the enchanted sea of The Odyssey, *it is not always possible to tell giants apart from living stones, or isles from wandering rocks; here, as Maryline Desbiolles wrote, "the landscape is a landscape that shifts."*

carefree life of a simple person." James Joyce likewise made him the prototype of a "good man, period." Ezra Pound portrayed him as the "average sensual man." More generally still, Moravia saw in Ulysses "a man [who] loves his wife and is not loved."

He prefers the lovely, lush countryside, richly decorated houses, opulent cities with "harbors, shapely ships and squares filled with heroes," and "tall and mighty ramparts crowned by their palisades," over the "infertile sea." But he likes nothing as much as the great Mediterranean sway of toil and scrub. He knows no refuge more welcoming than the tangled branches "of a wild olive and a cultivated olive." A man of diversity, he feels at home in the Mediterranean's many different landscapes. He likes the stony dales of the island where he was born, as well as the "soft meadows of parsley and violets." His journey has taught him how to move transitionlessly from the bed of foliage and the dimmest cave to the bright lights of the palace of Alcinous, sparkling with gold and bronze enameled with blue, shining wood and fine shimmering fabrics.

Similarly, the heroes of *The Odyssey* do not move about within a homogeneous geographical area, contrary to what Victor Bérard wanted to show, nautical charts in hand. They move across several spaces, some of which are real, like Telemachus' journey to Pylos and Sparta, and Menelaus' seven-year visit to Cyprus, Phoenicia and all the peoples of Egypt, Arabia and Ethiopia, not forgetting Libya "where lambs are born with horns." Other destinations, on the other hand, are nowhere lands like Ulysses' forays to the Cicones, the Lotus-eaters, the land of the Cyclopes, the floating isle of Aeolus "encircled by an indestructible bronze wall and sheer walls of bare rock," and the island of Aeaea "where Circe lived," the misty lands of the Cimmerians, "on the boundaries of the Ocean," Hades, the isle of Thrinacia, "the wonderful island of the celestial sun..." Upon all these places, Ulysses cast a marvelling eye ("So now Ulysses gazed, motionless..."), describing the world in its invigorating brilliance, bathed in light, as if it were standing out against the even background of a vase with figures, like the garden of Alcinous:

> ... *surrounded by a wall lies a large orchard*
> *of four acres—pears and pomegranates, apple trees with glossy fruit,*
> *sweet figs and luxuriant olives.*

So we read *The Odyssey* with the sensation of seeing a nature which may be described in a clichéd way, but portrays the typical "Mediterranean landscape" forever and ever. In his first book, called *Birth of The Odyssey*, a sumptuous parody of Homer's poem, which he'd once thought of calling *Presence of the Mediterranean*, Giono locates his narrative in the environs of Marseilles and around Manosque: "I realized," he wrote in his preface, "that all the land round about, that beautiful juniper wool carpeting the hills, those country homes slumbering beneath their moaning cypresses, those washerwomen, bent over the wash tubs,

Istanbul-based novel *The Black Book*, Orhan Pamuk tells the tale of the imperial prince Osman Djêlâlettine who, haunted by the idea of "being able to be oneself," had the works of Voltaire, Shakespeare and Rousseau burnt; he also "had *The Thousand and One Nights* burnt, for its sultans who roamed their capital in disguise, and with whom he identified as a result of the book, no longer had anything in common with the sovereign the prince wished to become." All this notwithstanding, the *Nights*, as Malek Chebel wrote in *The Arab-Muslim Imaginary*, "are one of the cornerstones of the imaginary device of the Arab-Muslim civilization at its heights." Like *The Iliad* and *The Odyssey*, "the tales of Scheherazade make up a book that is a world, where the action has a marked effect, by way of its readers, on our representations of the Mediterranean. But unlike the Homeric epic, its coherence is fragile, subject to innumerable changes, split between several versions, as if the fortunes of the text added to the history of a literally infinite book the immense sequel of its re-readings. Legend has it that nobody can read the *Nights* cover to cover without dying. Inexhaustible versions of a narrative whose sources are themselves without number."

The series of tales is first mentioned in the 10th century in Mas'ûdî's *Fields of Gold*. The Persian and Indian collection of these "thousand extraordinary tales," which are the source of *Nights*, was very probably adapted to the Arab world under the caliphate of Hârûn al-Rachîd in the late 7th century. Scheherazade (who has a Persian name—Shahrazad) tells how she has striven to bring together some of their materials: "O lord of time, I have had mariners questioned on the quaysides of Baghdad and, in the caravansaris, camel drivers coming from Sudan and the land of Silk, and also your captains of police 'above board and under the table,' and thieves in their prison; and I have also seen fit to consult the white-bearded sheiks who read ancient writings: they have told me the story of dead cities buried beneath desert sands."

The *Nights* draw not only from the legends

78

of India and the chronicles of the kings and poets of Persia; they draw also from novels of chivalry, the fantastic tales of Cairo, and Hebrew and Chaldaean narratives. Stemming from the oral tradition, like the Homeric narrative, the *Nights* are also the masterpiece of the *mugun*, the erotic Arab genre indulged in of an evening among men of letters enjoying unfettered expression and sensual love at refined banquets. But nothing is said about its authors, imagined by some in the image of Scheherezade. According to the *Nights*, this latter "had read all manner of books and writings, and even went so far as to study works by sages and medical treatises. In her memory she had stored a host of poems and tales, she had learnt popular proverbs, philosophers' utterances and the maxims of kings. She was not content to be merely intelligent and wise; she had also to be educated and instructed in matters literary. As for the books she had read, it wasn't enough for her to have leafed through them: she had studied them all painstakingly."

The transcription of the *Nights*, undertaken first in Cairo and then in Baghdad in the 12th and 13th centuries, was the beginning of a saga which Galland's translation brought to a crucial pause. The story of the *Nights* then took off. In the 19th century, English, French and German publishers stepped up the number of their editions based on manuscripts printed in Calcutta (in 1814) and Cairo (in 1835). A new stage was overcome with the translation, which was published in the *Revue Blanche* between 1899 and 1904, by Doctor Mardrus, a connoisseur of the Orient brought up in Lebanon and Egypt. Drawing his inspiration from a 19th-century manuscript, called the "Bûlâq recension," which he declared he had followed word by word, Mardrus gave the *Nights* a translation that promised above all to be more faithful to the original than Galland's version, which he reproached for having sultans and the people of Baghdad talk "as if in Versailles or Marly." André Gide, who was a great admirer of Mardrus' *Nights*, confessed: "Galland was like the luke-warm steam room that comes before the really hot room in a hammam." Mardrus would actually reconstruct the *Nights* like no other translator, indulging in a complete reinvention when the Bûlâq edition seemed to him not to be "oriental" enough. Under his pen, keen never to be outdone by outrageous recipes, the merest "chicken stuffed with pistachios" changed into "those magnificent roast chickens, stuffed with pistachios, almonds, rice, raisins, pepper, cinnamon and minced mutton." Mardrus was forever adding things, as if the initial text clamoured to be "stuffed" again and again with new ingredients, to make it more flavorful. It wasn't enough to translate "stuffed aubergine." In order to actually offer a taste of the stuffing, he was bound to specify that "everything about it was arranged with the skill of expert fingers: minced lamb, chick-peas, pine nuts, cardamom seeds, nutmeg, cloves, ginger, pepper and aromatic herbs." The English translator of the *Nights*, Sir Richard Burton, attributed Mardrus with the translation of a "mysterious authentic manuscript which he wrote himself;" his *Nights* still cast a stronger spell than many a recent transcription, more than a few of which seem surprisingly adrift.

Two scrupulous translations show no less surprising discrepancies. In his 1986 translation, René Khawam describes the Lady shopping in the market at the fruit- and flowermonger: "She bought pale-colored apples,

quinces from Turkey, peaches from Khoullane, musk-scented apples, jasmine, Syrian water lilies, slender cucumbers, lemons from Marahib, royal citrons, white roses, basil, henna flowers, fresh camomile, wallflowers, lilies-of-the-valley, ordinary lilies, anemones, violets, yellow-petaled bull's-eye daisies, narcissi, and pomegranate flowers." The same passage by André Miquel, in 1991, turns the pale-colored apples into Syrian applies the Turkish quinces come from Oman, the jasmine from Aleppo, the water lilies from Damascus, the fine cucumbers from the Nile, the lemons from Marahib are from Egypt, the myrtle has turned into a white rose and mignonettes, daisies and buttercups, missing from the bunch of flowers in the Khawam version now appear... "Then she goes to the dried fruit vendor where she takes a little bit of everything," André Miquel then notes, while René Khawam lists "pistachio hearts—delicious to nibble when

80

you're having a drink in good company—raisins from Chibb, almond nuts, dried dates from Iraq, Baalbek walnut biscuits, chick-peas from Khazaïne." Loose renderings of the *Nights*, where Galland's characters sleep whereas the same couples, in Mardrus' version, fornicate until first light! The *Nights* still intrigue and spellbind us, because of the very instability of these endless variants. People have often compared the Koran, that divine text handed down in its perfection—*ne varietur*—to us today, which orthodox theologians forbid in translation for reasons of sacrilege and gross betrayal, with the largely pre-Islamic *Nights*, which are no more than translations, endless tales of tales, a triumph of the word—which saves life—over the sultan's murderous decrees. The contrast between the two works nevertheless operates within a culture of oral tradition and the embellishments of a magic word, where the two Mediterraneans meet.

"But how does one learn how to tell stories to please a king?" asks the young harem girl
described by Fatima Mernissi in Dream of Women.
Like the painter, the photographer composes his picture with the help of details that, so we believe,
say it all about the East.

Don Quixote

In *Desire for Spain*, his beautiful book about walks in Spain, one rainy day Cees Nooteboom takes *la rota de Don Quixote*, the Don Quixote trail, which traces a hesitant loop to the southwest of Madrid. The journey begins with a stop in Chinchon, renowned for its ellipsoidal Plaza Major, then proceeds through Consegrua, site of the episode with the windmills, Almagro, for which Miguel de Cervantes had little time, El Toboso, homeland of Dulcinea, and the castle of Belmonte, not forgetting Argamasilla de Alba, where the writer was imprisoned, and then ending up at Alcala de Herrares, the town where he was born.

Cees Nooteboom is not some new-fangled Victor Bérard following in the steps of Rocinante and his master like the philologist hero of *The Odyssey* around the Mediterranean, in search of the real geography of the ingenious hidalgo's adventures. Nooteboom is aware that Cervantes' La Mancha is a paper landscape of places whose only basis in reality is a written one: a village, an inn, a main thoroughfare, hermitages, fields, a cool dale, a wild mountain. With the exception of a few unusual places—Don Diego's house, the duke's castle, the cave of Montesinos and Barcelona—Don Quixote rambles who knows where in a land befitting a chivalric romance, where it is best not to linger too long. He is scarcely more certain about the place he finds himself in than he is about his own identity, roaming as he does without maps or money. His adventures, as he tells Sancho, "are not island adventures," but crossroads, where Rocinante leads his fellow along as dictated by the muddle of names, like so many quid pro quos that have him mistaking the commander of a fortress for a hotelier, a gentlewoman for a whore, and one place for another.

This apparent indifference to places and landscapes, all mixed together in an inextricable hodgepodge, doesn't mean that Cervantes was not sensitive to them. All that mattered in *Don Quixote de la Mancha* was their generalness, like the landscapes in Kafka's *America*. Yet Cervantes was an experienced traveller who journeyed through Italy, sailed the Mediterranean, was held prisoner in Algiers, and was forced to crisscross Castile as a tax collector. *Voyage to Parnassus*, *La Galatea* and *Exemplary Stories* all certainly contain descriptions of the Mediterranean. Whence his sense of wonder upon seeing Genoa "covered with decorative gardens, white houses and towers with sparkling spires which, when struck by sun beams, bounced back such amazing rays that it was almost impossible to look at them." In *The Glass Licensee*, he extols the "beauty of the city of Naples, the delights of Palermo, the abundance of Milan, the celebrations of Lombardy, and many a splendid hotel meal." With a plethora of savoury details, he draws up a list of Italian wines, in which we find "the smoothness of the Trebbian, the virtue of the Montefiascone, the vigor of the Esperin, the generosity of the Viti, the mild affability of Miss Guarnache, the rusticity of the Centola." As he points

Don Quixote, 1868–1870, Honoré Daumier.
Don Quixote does not travel in La Mancha but decides, as Cervantes wrote,
to set sail in the ocean of books, "through the vast world, with his steed and his arms, in search of adventures,
to put into practice everything he had read about what errant knights did."

out in *The Trials of Persiles and Sigismunda*, in Rome, where he was in the service of cardinal Acquaviva, "he saw everything, admired everything, appreciated everything just so." As for Naples, where he stayed in the year of the battle of Lepanto, in "the best city in Europe and even in the whole world," but where he had to suffer "ill treatment from bugs, petty theft by convicts, the annoyances of mariners, the ravages of rats and the exhausting battering of the sea," he was the happiest of mortals.

Unlike Cervantes, Don Quixote does not travel, he wanders around a landscape of nowhere. He slips away into his imagination. His expeditions are spasmodic, lasting sometimes for two days, sometimes eighteen. They all lead him into either a wilderness or a labyrinth. In his *Entorno al casticismo*, Unamuno described Castile the way it looms forth in *Don Quixote*... It's a uniform, monotonous landscape with its contrasts of light and shadow, and its bold hues offer few nuances. The land itself comes across like a huge expanse of mosaic, endlessly the same, or almost, above which the very intense blue of the sky stretches into the distance. The landscape of the narrative is a "petrified sea, filled with sky," usually uninhabited, or lived in by Moors in the fields, dotted by squalid farms with only a little donkey and a few chickens, dreadful inns, highways with merchants going from Toledo to Seville, Galician wheeler-dealers,

84

[Above] Sicily, Bruce Davidson.

[Facing] Windmills at Alcazar de San Juan, in southern Spain.
*Don Quixote isn't very sure that he's called Don Quixote, nor that he's travelling in the right country;
in his confusion, he meets characters who look like landscapes, and windmills which he takes for knights.*

corpses being conveyed from Baeza to Segovia, and lords on their way to Aragon and Andalusia. The Spain of *Don Quixote* doesn't stay put. On his third excursion, Don Quixote goes to Barcelona by way of Saragossa, across the region of Villahermosa. Barcelona seems to him "the abode of courtliness, refuge of foreigners, hospital of the poor, homeland of the valiant, haven for the injured, a hub shared by every manner of sincere amity, in the world's loveliest site." The city is depicted through its *ramblas*, its port, its nightlife and its youthfulness, all ingredients which recur in many a present-day description of the city. But what catches Cervantes' attention most of all is the throng of fictional and romantic characters he encounters: the Basque, the Andalusian, the Castilian, the Aragonese, all interest him more than Barcelona itself. Like the hidalgo and the duenna, they represent a richer novelistic material than the city's monuments. But these characters are no more real than the stereotypical setting in which Cervantes puts them. "We are in such a strange world that living in it is just like a dream, and experience teaches me that the person who lives dreams what he is, until such time as he awakes. The king dreams that he is king and, by living in his illusion, he rules, he decrees and he governs... What is life? An illusion, a shadow, an invention, a fiction, and the greatest good is next to naught, for the whole of life is a dream and dreams are just dreams."

Narratives

Italian Journey

Some are tourists, others travellers. The former readily imagine they are the latter. But for the latter, to be taken for the former is a fate worse than death. On a study trip to Luxor in 1819, the Count of Forbin, director of museums, was even then irked by the incongruous presence of tourists in the terrain of the learned traveller: "I endlessly bumped into an English chambermaid in a wee pink-colored jacket, clutching a parasol," he wrote, at the end of his tether, in his *Journey to the Levant*, ushering in—as pointed out by Jean-Claude Berchet in his preface to the collection titled *The Voyage to the Orient*, what would "become a same old story...of travel literature": the traveller's lament and that of his untimely double.

"In Italy I am travelling in England," wrote Stendhal in his *Journal Litteraire*. More harshly, Chateaubriand noted in his *Mémoires d'Outre-Tombe*: "De Brosses depicts the English on the Piazza di Spagna the way we see them today, living together, making a whole lot of noise, looking at wretched human beings from head to toe, and heading back to their reddish hovels in London without having cast scarcely a glance at the Coliseum." We find the same rebuke issuing from Julien Gracq about American tourists in the Rome of his book *Around the Seven Hills*, "isolated from the microbial culture of the Mediterranean native by some invisible gauze." All that Barrès saw in the advent of tourism was "herds of innocents." In the very first pages of his Mediterranean journey, as described in *The Pillars of Hercules*, Paul Theroux stigmatizes tourists on the rock of Gibraltar, and vows to turn his back on them until the very last day. It turns out to be anything but a simple exercise, because the very first thing in which the tourist takes delight is, precisely, appearing in the frame, showing himself, existing, taking photographs and being photographed *in situ*—in a nutshell, laying claim, whenever the opportunity arises, to his share of visibility.

The traveller's attitude is another thing altogether. Jacques Lacarrière would say that it is akin to an "exercise of disappearance." Whereas the tourist displays on his T-shirt his membership of the world he has just left, the traveller is seeking a fantastical merger with the country being travelled across. True travellers have been disguising themselves for a long time: Byron, Nerval, Flaubert, Burton, Loti, Rimbaud, Isabelle Eberhardt and Lawrence: the list of Oriental impersonators is a lengthy one. Yet the distinction between the two categories is less straightforward than it might seem. Travel writers describe many a way of journeying in and around the Mediterranean, and return home with a huge variety of reports.

One of the first was Michel de Montaigne, who wrote up his *Italian Journey*, which kept him away from home—and his "dreaming...library"—for all of eighteen months, between 1580 and 1581. Reading him today is a treat.

86

Capri at Daybreak, 1836, Carl Morgenstern (detail).
The approach to the sea, "along a rocky path."

[Pages 88–89] *View of the Farnese Gardens, Rome*, 1826, Jean-Baptiste-Camille Corot.
What would the Roman countryside be for us if Corot and Chateaubriand hadn't made it the masterpiece of all Mediterranean landscapes?

mars 1826

Partly dictated to a secretary, partly penned by his own hand, written in Italian and French, the manuscript was discovered quite by chance in a trunk in La Brède castle in 1770. It was published four years later. Accompanied by four gentlemen and half a dozen servants, Montaigne headed to Italy for a change of air; he was also keen to take the waters, tend to his "stony health" (he was suffering from kidney stones), mourn the death of Etienne de La Boétie, have a holiday after the publication of the *Essays*, and find freedom from the "duties of marital friendship." Above all, however, it was his intent to practice "the exercitation of [his] soul," observe the "different customs," for "the pleasure of visiting unknown lands," even if he would not be leaving "Christianity."

Since the mid-16th century, travel to Italy was once again possible. The peace treaty of Cateau-Cambrésis had just been signed; the *pax hispanica* reigned over the peninsula; the road was less fraught with risk. Montaigne started out by witnessing the siege of La Fère (in northeastern France), then took the road to the Alps, which he crossed via the Brenner Pass; he then proceeded to Verona, Vicenza and Padua, and stayed in Venice before undertaking a slow return journey to Bordeaux, by way of Florence, Bologna, Rome and Siena. To guide him, he had at his beck and call a wealth of travel literature, with which he would not burden himself, nor attempt to reproduce in any way. "I shall consider all things most particularly," he wrote. "I would try to portray them here, but there are public books and paintings on this subject." His narrative would take another avenue, one dictated to him by its "poetic allure," "returning very often close to where he had set out," as his secretary noted, for he had "no plan but to wander." His companions reproached him for "changing opinions as the occasion demanded," but he didn't mind; he had elected to travel "along the byways," which at times meant undertaking, in one go, a ten-hour stretch on horseback "no matter how colic he might be." Nothing would prevent him from going "in leaps and bounds" where his delightful roaming led him. So it was with a heavy heart indeed that he resolved to return to Bordeaux, where the office of mayor awaited him.

Italy had not exhausted his desire to still see and marvel at inventions of the "unusual," born again like the "plashing of an infinity of springs" from the Tivoli fountains. Montaigne's *Italian Journey* was probably the first of the Grand Tours, undertaken with the sole purpose of savoring the curiosities and oddities of the Mediterranean world. Jacques Lacarrière lends his journeys a definition which the author of the *Essays* would not have contradicted: "Isn't travelling," he says, "like wasting one's time in the most enchanted way, as substantially as possible … Feeling a closeness to those Faraway and a kinship with those who are Different?" Montaigne, with his curiosity about everything and anything, went to Italy without any particular religion; without his travelling companions, "he would rather have gone to Krakow or Greece." Free to consider things and people "at his leisure"; a "whore" and a prelate, a crowd and a "cabman" alike, a landscape and a fountain-maker's invention, all bestirred him equally. His happiness lay in the "diverse" that turned its back on plans, "the extravagant," the unforeseen "wrong end of the stick." He was well removed from the idea of seeing everything the way the 17th-century English "grandtourist" was recommended to see things, transformed, as he was, into a methodical investigator of an Italy that was inspected and described down to the tiniest detail. And the learned observation that would offer a pretext for many an 18th-century journey, too, was not what obsessed him either, any more than did works of art and monuments. Chateaubriand was amazed to see Montaigne regard "St. Peter's like a sparrows' nest hanging in the forecourt of the Coliseum."

Johann Wolfgang von Goethe's *Italian Journey* (1786–1788) was similar to Montaigne's in many respects. Like Montaigne, Goethe set off for the "land of flowering lemon trees" without any fixed schedule, merely eager to get away from the court of Duke Carl August in Weimar (to whom he was "private counsellor") and the glacial Charlotte von Stein. Like Montaigne, too, his interests were as varied as could be. If he steered a course towards a "world of magnificent images," he also set off in order to devote himself to studies of botany, mineralogy, geology and climatic analysis. His research into the "secret of the design and organization of plants" and on "the supersensitive primordial plant," as he described it in a letter to Herder, and on primitive stones, would find fertile terrain in Italy. Was it not the land of gardens, earthquakes and volcanic eruptions? His climbs up Vesuvius gave him every bit as much as his visits to churches. There was a equal interest in all his areas of research: the primitive model would enable him to understand the history of forms in the vast "garden of the world." But the crux of his journey lay elsewhere: "For me," he wrote to Charlotte, "all that matters is the impressions of the senses." In Italy, the man of the Enlightenment was constantly overwhelmed by the *Augenmensch*, the beholding man, "the man born to see," who once more found pleasure in the perceptible presence of the world in the light of the South (the *Midi* or *Mezzogiorno*), when in contact with masterpieces. "In the Church of the Hermits," he wrote, "I saw paintings of Mantegna, one of the painters of the old school, which filled me with amazement. What a sure and precise presence in those canvases!...An absolutely true presence, not by apparent example, whose effort would be illusory, addressing solely the imagination, but harsh, pure, clear, luminous, conscientious, and delicate, at the same time as having something austere, laborious and painful." Goethe's *Italian Journey*, which was published long after Montaigne's *Italian Journey*, described neither an encyclopaedist's journey nor an antiquarian's sojourn: in Italy, Goethe practised "the intoxicated oblivion of oneself" which would turn him into a "new man."

When Stendhal crossed the Alps for the first time in 1800, in the wake of Napoleon's armies, he was 17. On his very first evening in Novara, he hastened to the theatre. They were performing Cimarosa's *The Secret Marriage*. Mistress Caroline had "one tooth less at the front" but the show, in that place, after a day of ordeal by fire, thrilled him. He noted in his diary: "My life was revitalized and all my disappointment about Paris buried forever. I had just clearly seen where happiness lay." Two conditions were brought together: "living in Italy and hearing that music." Next stop, wealthy Lombardy. The beauty of the landscape, the dense verdant green as far as the eye could see. When he reached Milan, he found everything just to his liking: a handsome stairway, a drawing room, the architecture of the Casa Adda where he was staying, breadcrumb-coated cutlets. It was, he wrote, "the most beautiful time of my life." And then he wiled away his days "in the most beautiful place on Earth." Eleven years later, he was back in Milan, on his own this time around, for the sheer pleasure of being in Italy, "admiring everything"—"coffee with cream and delicious ice cream," the streets of Milan "so perfectly clean," the dull sound

of carriages on the stone thoroughfares amid the cobblestones, the Guido Renis in the Brera, the disposition of the Milanese, La Scala, where he immediately headed on his first evening back and every night thereafter. In Rome, the social circle of Duchess Lante enthralled him more than the ruins.

In 1803, Chateaubriand also made his own Italian journey. Like Stendhal, as he made his way through Lombardy, he gazed in wonder at the sight of such throngs of peasants and laborers "barefoot, and wearing large straw hats" who were "scything the meadows, cutting the cereal crops, singing, leading teams of oxen, and rowing boats up and down the water-courses." Italy was like a Poussin painting. Chateaubriand's destination was Rome, and the embassy of Cardinal Fesch. "I am overwhelmed," he wrote to his friend Joubert, "persecuted by what I have seen; what a city! what memories!" The anguished weight of this initial reaction (the diametric opposite of Stendhal's buoyant jubilation in Milan) would leave its mark on the *Italian Journey* that he would publish on his return. On July 16th, he wrote thus to Molé: "If you saw that great solitude of the Roman countryside, the Tiber flowing almost unexplored within its abandoned banks, you would be struck, as I was, by this single idea that follows me everywhere, the nothingness of human things." Rome provided the young Chateaubriand with the stuff for meditating on collapsing empires, ruin following ruin, and the notion of tempus fugit. The bravura, "purple" passage in all this was his *Letter to Fontanes*, which would help to establish the myth of the "Roman countryside" for a long time to come: "You will find just a few trees, he wrote, but everywhere there are ruined aqueducts and tombs; ruins which seem to be the forests and the native plants of a land made up of the dust of the dead and the rubble of empires." The Roman countryside was a fossilized landscape. In it, Antiquity was at once intact—"these fields are such as they have been left by the ploughshare of Cincinnatus and the last Roman cart"—and in ruins.

Views of the Forum, 1996.
"The world doesn't start with Rome; nor does it end with Rome.
The Mediterranean likewise. And the Mediterranean isn't Rome," wrote Gabriel Audisio,
as a fierce foe of the Latin sea of between-the-wars extreme rightwing ideologies.

Returning to Rome in 1828 to assume his ambassadorial duties, Chateaubriand devoted less time to daydreaming about ruins and Rome's "exteriors" than to Roman society. Rome was no longer the barren landscape of his first impressions, the color of ash and dust, but a theatre with some remarkable actors in it. Of Leo XII, who duly received him, he said that "he hardly eats; he lives, with his cat, on a little polenta," and of Cardinal Vidoni that he was "fat and tall, with a glowing face and his cap askew"; of a Portuguese ambassador that he was "a misshapen dwarf, restless, grimacing, green like a Brazilian monkey and yellow like a Lisbon orange"; and, lastly, of his friend the painter Guerin, that he lived "withdrawn, like a sick dove, at the top of a pavilion in the Villa Médicis." Chateaubriand read French travellers: Rabelais' writings, finding their way into Jean du Bellay's luggage in 1536, Montaigne, Coulanges, de Brosses, Misson and Lalande. Since his *Letter to Fontanes*, he was quite sure that "there had been a shift from disparagement to enthusiasm," and that he had made a considerable contribution thereto. His only great predecessors were Poussin and Claude Lorrain. Thenceforth, he strove to depict Rome from the inside. A "dark" *miserere* in the Sistine Chapel: "The candles snuffed out one after the other releasing from their stifled light a faint white smoke, a fairly natural image of life compared by the Scriptures to a little vapor," or alternatively the "waves of beauties, diamonds, flowers and feathers" of a reception at the Villa Medicis. The picture of ruins had given way to the music of the *Mémoires*. Before long, Chateaubriand left Rome; he would be followed by countless literary pilgrims, describing their despondency and their enthusiasm. But at the very same time Rome was indeed a fairy tale, an indolent promenader's dream, a treasure trove of squares "into which you unforeseeably slip as if into the central area of a maze" splashed by the "unexpected watery witching hour" of a Baroque fountain.

A Burgundian through his father Henri VI, the Germanic emperor, and attached to Lower Lorraine and Normandy through his mother, Constance d'Hauteville, the posthumous daughter of the brilliant Roger II of Sicily, Frederick would live among the Arabs, the Jews, the Spanish, the Blacks, the Egyptians, the Germans and the Italians who reached the quaysides of the Golden Conch at Palermo, forever borrowing from them all. Ernst Kantorowicz invites us, in his monumental monograph, to follow Frederick step by step: "Without supervision, the young king, aged eight or nine, roamed through the markets and gardens of his half-African capital, at the foot of the Pellegrino, in that place where, in a welter of disconcerting multicolored patterns, peoples and religions and customs all mingled together. Minarets of mosques and cupolas of synagogues rubbed shoulders there with Norman churches and cathedrals that Byzantine overlords had in their turn embellished with gilded mosaics, and whose structures were supported by Greek columns on which Saracens had engraved the name of Allah in Kufic characters."

As king of Sicily, duke of Apulia, prince of Capua and king of the Romans, Frederick learnt algebra, geometry and mathematics. "Before assuming the responsibilities of power," he wrote, "I sought Knowledge and inhaled its balsamic scent." He also trained in the handling of weapons and military strategy, and visited shipbuilding yards; sailors taught him oceangoing navigation; he talked with engineers and architects, showed an interest in the grooming of horses and how to tend exotic animals, and developed a keen passion for the art of falconry; he consulted herbaria, wrote poems, spoke Greek, Latin, Arabic, Provençal and Sicilian. Constance of Aragon, whom he married in 1208, taught him courtly manners. In 1220, he was crowned in Rome, by Pope Honorius III, head of the Holy Roman Empire, clad in gold-embroidered crimson silk like the Byzantine *Basilei*, swathed in a purple cloak adorned with a palm tree and rampant lions. He was 26 years old. He reigned over the greatest Empire that Europe had known since Charlemagne. He was the new Caesar, "perpetually august and unvanquished," "*stupor mundi*," as people would duly say, too. His curly chestnut-red hair, his greenish-blue eyes, his vivaciousness, and his intellectual inquisitiveness all stood him apart, despite his small stature, which would not have made a high-priced slave of him. Fra Salimbene, a lesser monk, described him thus: "He was wily, shrewd, sparing, sensual, mean and given to fits of anger. Yet he was at times a courageous man; he could be benevolent, lighthearted and delightful when he wished to show friendliness and courtesy. He was active, could read, write and sing, compose songs and music. He was a healthy-looking, well-made man, though of average height. I set eyes upon him and he pleased me a great deal. He could speak several languages and had he been a good Catholic and had he loved God, the Church and his own soul, few emperors could have rivalled him in the world."

The portrait doesn't shrink from the main rebuke: too many mixed cultures could not turn the emperor into a good Christian, and the company of philosophers and scholars of all manner of origin was the proof of a naturally impious mind. When he set off—reluctantly—on a Crusade, it was in the company of his

[Page 106] Untitled, 1993, Jean-Charles Blais.

[Page 107] Alexander the Great (356–323 BCE).
There is no greater conqueror figure than that of Alexander, nor Mediterranean more triumphant.
"When Napoleon landed in Egypt, wrote B. Porcel, the Bedouin believed that Alexander was returning:
his legend has never died among the peoples encountered by the Macedonian."

"magna curia," his court of poets, scholars and learned men with whom he would argue nightly over issues that haunted him and made him "greatly amazed": What do angels do all the time in the presence of God? How does the earth hold itself in space? What is the original language of mankind? How are we to explain explosions? The shape of stones? The eternity of the soul? These were all matters which he also discussed in his letters, and which exercised him more than the liberation of the Holy Land. Yet he achieved this latter with the Treaty of Jaffa in 1229, without having gone into battle.

On his return to Sicily, he built castles and triumphal arches which strike the imagination by the omnipotence of their geometry and the brand of Roman authority that emanates therefrom. One of the best preserved of them is the Castel del Monte, "crown of Apulia." Built on a peak in the Murge, not far from Barletta, it rises above the coastal lowlands in the distance and the vastness of the hinterland. Modeled on the Dome of the Rock, which had left such a powerful impression on him in Jerusalem, he apparently designed this massive "folly" himself, made up, as it was, of a double concentric octagon flanked without by eight octagonal towers. The interior, stripped of the pink marble from Brescia, the ceramics covering it and the rich furnishings that originally decorated it, takes the breath away, such is the total sway of the geometric order therein. In fact you have to imagine this "dream of stone" lined within by silks and rugs and surrounded by a tent village. A kind of mobile town which accommodated the emperor's escort. A town ready to pull up stakes and go to other sites: the fortress of Lucera, in particular, which Frederick II had built to house the Arab colony in Sicily, Maniaco at Syracuse, Castel Ursino at Catania, the Jebel Seiss in Syria, and others still at Melfi and Messina. Even if he made Foggia and the Capitanate his capital in 1211, Frederick II was forever on the move.

Contemporaries described the incredible caravan "of apes and ivory" that accompanied him on his great travels: around the emperor, in hunter's garb on Dragon, his black steed, they give us a glimpse of the court, the cohort of the Arab guard, the host of pages, the Teutonic knights, the prelates, the musicians, the swarm of dogs harnessed in pairs, falconers and their hobbled snow leopards followed by soldiers, servants and maids and the imperial menagerie, where you could see giraffes, elephants, black bears and exotic fowl. The Pope, for his part, reproached this sultan's caravanserai where you looked around for a harem behind the cages. But Frederick went on just the same. One of the works which he paid meticulous attention to was a treatise on falconry for his son Manfred, with a precision and a technicality worthy of the Renaissance man he was, ahead of his time. On his death, in 1250, he was embalmed in accordance with the Egyptian rite, in a dalmatic vestment embroidered in gold thread with a verse from the Koran in Kufic script and a purple cloak, a sword decorated with Arabic inscriptions on the side, laid out in a coffin of porphyry embellished by two Sassanid lions.

Figures

The Odalisque

As the masterpiece of the Oriental Eros, the odalisque is the depiction and representation of a realized fantasy—that of the woman destined for the bedchamber (*odalik* in Turkish literally means "for the bedroom"), spreadeagled over cushions, waiting upon her master's pleasure. The way the theme has been treated since the 18th century is associated with depictions of the harem: the odalisque is not merely the beautiful slave woman, languid and unveiled: she embodies in the western imagination the role of the captive surprised in the seraglio.

Through its presentation, the odalisque literally depicts an order of desire, as in Ingres' *Odalisque and Slave* (1838), on view in the museum at Cambridge and duplicated by the painter—with the help of Flandrin, 43 years later!—in the Baltimore version. The odalisque is surrounded by all the accessories of the "bedchamber": the water-pipe, the fan, the incense-burner, and ritual gifts from the sultan. But the crux lies in the subtle gradations which confine the characters concerned within a thoroughly codified ritual: that of the black eunuch—absent body, part of the décor— the singing half-caste female slave (the *qaïna*) playing the *tchégour* (the female musician slave had a lofty rank in the seraglio: trained from girlhood in Damascus or Baghdad, her price was a hundred times higher than that of a captive female with no musical skills), offering to the beholding eye the odalisque's beauty, even as she sang of it. For the bedchamber itself, opening onto a pond and the leafy plants of a garden, Ingres drew his inspiration from the detailed description made of the seraglio in Istanbul by Lady Montagu: "One entered a marble-floored vestibule, the design of which formed the loveliest mosaic. From there, one proceeded to a bedchamber surrounded by sofas, on which one could rest before entering the bath...Around this bed, there were little gold dishes burning with the mildest aromatic spices of the Orient, and it was there that several women destined to this employ waited on their own as they got out of the bath to dry their beautiful bodies and rub in the gentlest of essences; it was there that she would then have a voluptuous rest."

Gérôme and Chassériau, Manet with his *Olympia* (1863), as well as Bazille, Renoir, Cézanne and even Matisse in the 1920s, would all deal with this theme. So its amazing career was understandably full of surprises. With the war over, what prompted Matisse to deal with a subject that belonged to 19th century painting? "Yes, I needed to breathe," he explained to André Verdet, "to give in to repose and a sensual oblivion, far from Paris. The odalisques were the fruit both of a happy nostalgia, a lovely, living dream,

Grande Odalisque à la Culotte Bayadère, 1925, Henri Matisse.
The period of the odalisques: "Everywhere characterized," wrote Aragon,
"by that nonchalance we find in Ingres."

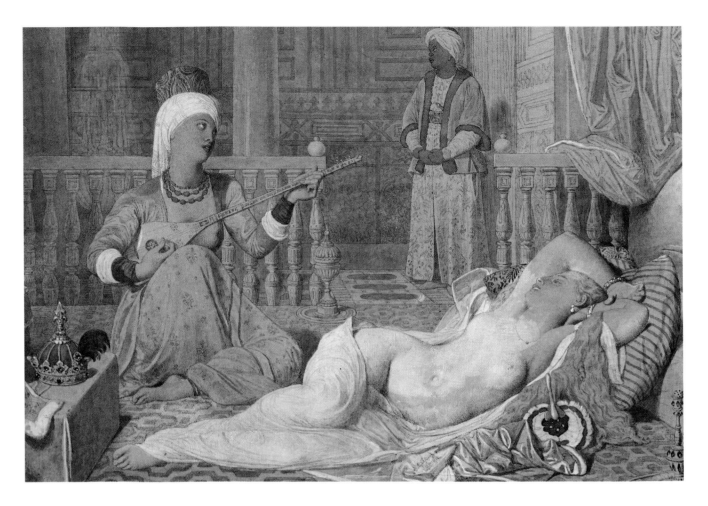

and a demand lived almost in the ecstasy of days and nights, in the spell of a climate." But what kind of nostalgia was involved? Thoughts of his stay in Tangiers in 1912 and 1913? The painting of Ingres and Delacroix? Prewar days? Or an imaginary Orient which Nice, with its Moorish villas and its fantasy Alhambras recreated like a cinema set? By remaking a decorative Orient—in a bedchamber—, Matisse produced an intentionally artificial work. The Odalisque is another name for designating the picture, that decorative object which is sufficient unto itself. And at the same time Matisse turned the Mediterranean into an ornamental make-believe that relegated its real presence to the background, in the oval of a mirror or the cracks of half-open shutters. Odalisques are the preordained figures of an allegorical Orient that the late works would only represent in this decorative and monumental form: running counter to the real Mediterranean which Matisse could glimpse from his windows.

[Above] *Odalisque and Slave*, 1858, J.A.D. Ingres.

[Facing] Portrait of a young woman, Morocco.

[Pages 114–115] *The Massage*, 1883, Edouard-Bernard Debat-Ponsan.
"Oh, how hot it was!": the bath, that pretext for the erotic unveiling of countless orientalist pictures titled In the Hammam, Massage, Harem Scene. *"The Orient does not really look like itself," wrote Alain Buisine, "it only really conforms to its own image when it starts to look like a pictorial image of the Orient."*

E. DEBAT-PONSAN
1883

Figures

The Peasant

The image of Virgil's laborer who "passes prosperous days" and "tills the field tilled by his forefathers," that field which "fed the State, his children, his flocks and his oxen, companions in his happy labors," has for a long time dominated the classical iconography of the Mediterranean peasant. The peasant whom 18th- and 19th-century travellers expected and hoped to come upon on their way, in Italy, was precisely this. Stendhal and Chateaubriand in Lombardy and Campania described him, as did Poussin in his *Seasons*, in the midst of a pastoral landscape. In that same period, painters turned the Italian peasant into an idealized portrait, like Léopold Robert and his *Young Girl from Procida* (1822), clad in her regional costume, posing in front of a seaside landscape, looking for all the world like a rustic Mona Lisa or an ennobled peasant girl. German artists, who set off for Italy in Goethe's footsteps, also turned the peasant scene into an idyllic picture, such as Franz Cartel and his *Italian Shepherds* (1820) or his famous *Scene of Working-Class Life near Pozzuoli* (1823). Garish color prints and postcards disseminated the image of the Italian peasant woman for use by travellers making their Grand Tour. Picasso drew inspiration from this between 1917 and 1919 to put together his neoclassical effigies. Léopold Robert would also paint peasant festivities such as *The Return from the Pilgrimage to the Madonna of the Arch* (1827) and the *Arrival of the Harvesters in the Pontine Marshes* (1830). On his return from Italy, Corot would take up these archetypes of classical peasantry in his many Italian peasant girls and women with their dreamy beauty, bedecked in folkloric costumes, like *Agostina* (1866) and *Young Italian Girl* (1871), as would a great many academic painters such as Bouguereau with *Bringing Back the Harvest* (1878).

All these studio works freeze the image of the peasant, dressed for a festival or party, dancing against the backdrop of a sparkling sky, in a radiant landscape perched high above the sea. The peasant depicted by Van Gogh in Arles in the 1880s was no less idealized. To make him a feature of the Provençal countryside, a detour via Millet's work must be made. Van Gogh didn't paint the peasant of Arles, but the eternal harvester, the sheaf-binder, the sheep-shearer, the sower, the shepherdess from an reinvented world. An allegorical image that more realistic observers were already cruelly contradicting at the turn of the century: so in 1830 the reverend John Eustace emphasized "the frightening and repellent aspect of one or two rare peasants who lived in Campania: all the symptoms of dropsy, jaundice and malaria seemed to be brought together in their swollen bellies, their deformed features, their dark yellow complexion, their

116

livid eyes and lips." In his narrative of a Mediterranean journey, George Evans likewise worries about "depopulation, dying peasants, desolate villages and ruined hovels." In his *Italian Journey*, Taine was no less strident: "Their costumes are odd: old goat- or sheepskin jerseys, leather gaiters, bluish cloaks a hundred times drenched by rain, leather sandals as in primordial times, and rising from all this an unbearable smell. Their eyes are staring, blazing like those of an animal, brighter still and as if rendered savage shine forth the eyes of women yellow and weakened by fever." Travellers to the Orient were just as unkind with the Egyptian peasant glimpsed beside the road. In the 1890s, the farming crisis that struck Italy triggered an unprecedented wave of emigration, and gave rise to committed works such as G. Pelizza's *The Fourth Estate*: "A throng of laborers, the painter noted, clever, strong, tough, united, advancing like a torrent, tipping over everything in their way, thirsty for justice."

The peasants of Lucania, in southern Italy, as described by Carlo Levi in his magnificent book *Christ Stopped at Eboli* are, on the other hand, incapable of rising up, quite sure, as they are, that they are the "damned of the earth," forgotten by everyone else. If Christ didn't force on as far as Aliano (Gagliano in the book), it is, as one of the peasants declares, because: "We aren't Christians—Christian means, in their language, man—and that proverb I heard so often repeated is, in their mouths, merely the desolate expression of an inferiority complex: we aren't Christians, we aren't men, we aren't regarded as men but as beasts..." Put under house arrest by Mussolini in 1935 and 1936 in this long lost village amid the hills in this poorest of southern countrysides, Levi paints the portrait of a peasant world dominated by fear and quaint, old-fashioned rites, which a mutual hatred links to the class of the *galantuomini*, the small

[Pages 118–119] The Ruccolo family, in front of their house, Italy, 1946.
[From left to right] *The Arrival of the Reapers in the Pontine Marshes*, 1834–1835, Léopold Robert.
Andalusia, Spain.
Sheep, Provence.
The Mediterranean peasant between bucolic idealization
and the "anarchic and desperate" peasant civilization described by Carlo Levi.

landowners who hadn't managed to leave their homeland for Naples and Rome, and who "transform their own disappointment and their own mortal boredom into an overall rage..." The peasant of Aliano is the prototype of the mountain-dwelling farmer, the *cafone*, introverted (strong and silent), setting off at first light to till his inaccessible fields, and returning home in the evening, "back broken by fatigue and head humming from the sun," to a village now given over to goats and vermin. While the radiant image of the collective peasant toiling to build Fascism or Communism spread, the peasants depicted by Carlo Levi remain alien to history: "They don't nor can they have what is called a political consciousness, because they are, in the fully accepted sense of the term, pagans and not citizens," wrote Carlo Levi; "the gods of the State and the town cannot have their worship in those clayey lands where the wolf reigns along with the dark and ancient wild boar, where no wall separates the world of people from that of beasts and spirits, nor the visible branches of trees from the dark underground roots... They live immersed in a world with no determining features, where man is not distinct from his sun, his animals or his malaria; here there can be no happiness, as certain men of letters with a pagan bent dream of it, nor hope, for these are always individual sentiments; all that reigns here is the gloomy passiveness of a sorrowful nature."

Unlike Levi's characters, Giono's peasants are fictional, novelistic creations, "invented characters" in an "invented Provence" (like Van Gogh, Giono talks about Provence as if it were a country like Japan), living "invented histories," but they are no less marked by the seal of an immutable Mediterranean countryside subject to the same sorts of violence and the same poverty. With *Colline* (1929), Giono set a peasantry outside time, isolated from the world, evolving in a usually deserted universe, or one in the process of

121

emptying out, as in *Regain* (1930): "The people," he wrote in *Colline*, "are like islands in their little farms. They live, what's more, in a closed economy and they are almost all alone. They envy each other most of the time and hate one another." But, offsetting this imprisonment, Giono's peasants live "in the hollow of the world": "They are in contact with solitude and with the great cosmic forces: wind, rain, storms and even the architectonics of the landscape." In their struggle against their environment, they derive a strength which lends their fight an epic dimension. Unlike Levi's peasants, they are seeking happiness.

Giono refuses to see the peasant as someone straightforward: "The owner of an apple orchard, he notes, isn't the owner of an almond orchard. The huge horizons yield up one soul; the deep valleys and the narrow dales yield up another. The happiness being sought by the farmer with his lemons is a long way removed from the happiness that satisfies the farmer on stony plateaux in the midst of lavender fields." There is nothing more foreign to the writer than the standard figure of the "big mouth" Provençal man, "vain and frivolous," the way Alphonse Daudet and Joseph Méry have both caricatured him. What is striking, on the

other hand, in the host of novels is the extraordinary variety and the uniqueness of each one of the characters. And then the peasant is not alone. On Giono's Provençal byways, the lesser crafts of the Mediterranean world are innumerable: peddlers, healers, guitarists, conjurers, slightly wizard-like water-diviners, stray soldiers, anarchists, bird-watchers, cattle merchants, laundrywomen, cobblers, shady wheeler-dealers, churchless priests and landlubber mariners. And, again unlike Levi's Lucania, the novelist's Provence is crisscrossed by roads that are forever in motion, used by wanderers, bringing about all that history.

[Above] *Women at the Well* (opus 238), 1892, Paul Signac.

[Facing] Portrait of Jean Giono.
The writer at the time of The Great Flock *(1930) posing like a Virgilesque poet in
the huge cape worn by shepherds in Provence. The adventures of Angelo,
the Stendhalian hero of* The Horseman on The Roof, *would shift the image before very long.*

The Fisherman

The image of the Mediterranean fisherman is hard to define. In contrast to the oceangoing Atlantic fisherman—instantly recognizable in his boots and oilskin, braving the high seas in factory ships—the Mediterranean counterpart is more ambiguous. Depictions usually show him on land rather than caught up in the busyness of his activity, occupied with tiny tasks which, in Provence, are categorized as more or less invisible "lesser crafts." When a fishing sortie or a catch are filmed, it is during rare collective forays, and even more rarely on boats plying their way through the Strait of Gibraltar to join the fleet of "real fisherman." Images of the Mediterranean fisherman's day-to-day life are few and far between, as if his character were inexorably disappearing from the Mediterranean landscape. In his book about Alexandria, Daniel Rondeau observes the disproportion between the spectacle of a team of fishermen, roped together at the waist, helped by lads in swimming trunks, hauling ashore a long net, and the baskets of shrimps and prawns and sundry fish that are the end result. His presence in one or two ports and harbors where the "great craft" (fishing on the high seas) is still being carried on, is also tending to die out, replaced by a tourist icon of the seafaring fisherman, whose task is to bring to life a set from another time. Recently, a film called *Funny Felix* came up with an image of his boredom and solitude, saved by the rediscovery of friendship and kite-flying!

When Matisse painted *Luxe, calme et volupté* in 1904, after a summer spent with Signac in St. Tropez, he depicted the first seaside vacationers side by side with the boat of the *Poor Fisherman* borrowed from Puvis de Chavannes. The Mediterranean is a beach where fishermen coming straight from ancient mythology are still meant to come ashore. The following summer in Collioure, in *The Port of Abaill*, he actually depicted the fishermen at their daily activities and tasks, on the quayside, in a kind of sweeping view that might be said to be a sketch for a larger painting. But since then, and up until the end, the fisherman has been disappearing from the work, and not even be in Nice, where the painter lived on a beach where they still hauled ashore their nets, would the figure of the fisherman reappear. At L'Estaque, Cézanne didn't pay him any attention, nor did Renoir or Monet in their Mediterranean travels. Only Bonnard would keep a place for him, straying from his walks, back-lit, in the blue of the Bay of Cannes, as if he were part of the landscape. He loomed up on the shore invaded by bathers, the marginal silhouette of the old lead player, now a bit part in a vacation show.

If our depictions of the fisherman still persist, like the handsome "old man of the sea" of those between-the-wars postcards, they and he will also disappear in their turn. "The old fisherman," wrote Jean-Didier Urbain in *On the*

Sicilian fisherman.
The image of the "old fisherman": a cliché of the "eternal Mediterranean," with a hard life.

[Page 126] Sant'Elia, Palermo, 1978.

[Page 127] Fish merchant, 16th century BCE (late Minoan).
Images of octopuses. The deceptive images of a harvested sea.

Beach, "no longer stands his fishtraps on the strand; today they are made of moulded plastic and industrially manufactured. Nets made of cotton and hemp have been replaced by nylon nets; the old ones these days hang on restaurant walls." He is part of a folkloric tradition that is itself dying out. Paul Theroux wound up his tour of the Mediterranean without having met a single fisherman, apart from the director of a fish-farming establishment! The fisherman now appears in Mediterranean literature as a solitary figure, a stranger on the beach, sailing on the borderline of the world of holidays like someone in exile in his own land. Nicola, the fisherman in Erri De Luca's *You, Mine,* lives on his island (Ischia) out of time, in another world, not communicating at all with the horde of tourists who have invaded the island the way the Germans once did. But when the narrator comes upon him, he undertakes an apprenticeship—a kind of rite of passage towards adulthood—which is by no means limited to fishing. In Jean-Claude Izzo's first thriller, *Total Khéops,* he describes fishing, towards Les Goudes, in the very direst moments of the story, as the haven of his hero Fabio Montale. In the loveliness of the Bay of Marseilles, "immersing oneself in the sea" is like breathing a little and learning once again how to live.

In any event, fishermen are different; they are, as Yachar Kemal notes in *Salih the Wonderstruck,* "different from other men, they don't look like everybody else, especially not those big-bellied types involved in buying and selling things." Their world is partly bound up with the high seas and the night, even when they don't sail far from the shore and no longer very often practice lamp-fishing. Even if it's a very long time since fishing with fire, as was practiced in the Middle Ages, and is no longer a significant activity of the Mediterranean's, the night is still the time of the fisherman. It is synonymous with a struggle with devilish powers. In 1939, with *Night-fishing at Antibes,* Picasso devoted to it a picture: the fisherman, armed with his pronged harpoon ready to surprise the fish attracted by the light, and spear his prey. It is quite a long time, too, since tuna-fishing has really galvanized the throng of fisherman in those spectacular fights. Has the Mediterranean of the small catch also laid down its arms?

[Above] The corniche, at Alexandria.
What city to choose? The huge, dusty cement-covered coastal suburbs wedged between sea and lagoon, the archaeological treasure with its recent inventions, or the paper city of Durrell and Cavafy?

[Facing] Tuna-fishermen in Spain.
"The powerful creatures, many of which are the same size as men, gleaming and blood-spattered, made me think," wrote Paul Valéry, "of men-at-arms whose dead bodies had been brought ashore. That was a painting of a somewhat epic grandeur that I readily called "Return from the Crusades."

Figures

The Bather

The fisherman has become removed from our representations of the Mediterranean, where he survives, proudly alone, in a landscape which no longer requires his presence. Since the late 19th century, the bather has replaced him on these shores which might be said to have been colonized by seaside vacationing. Up until then, his image was not particularly present in depictions of the Inland Sea. Ulysses was not fond of bathing. When he did happen to swim, it was because he was forced to by a shipwreck, in the dangerous backwash of some cove or creek. Nor did Nausicaa, who preferred the fresh waters of rivers to the beaches of the kingdom of Alcinous. The diver of Thera, or the image of the fisherman clutching bunches of fish in his hands, are glowing exceptions which cause us to imagine other kinds of bathing. The Romans who rushed headlong in the summer months to the beaches of Ostia, and had villas built at Baiae, Cumae and Misenum, and on the beaches of Latium, were fond of the sea, but there are few depictions showing them actually swimming. During his Italian journey, Goethe was one of the rare people to observe the dozen swimmers who were paid by Sir William Hamilton to put on for him, every afternoon from his terrace, a spectacle which the Baron von Gloeden would certainly not have missed.

The presence of the bather in the Mediterranean, in the age of "sea bathing," echoed the vogue of Atlantic beaches. It did not become pronounced until the 1920s. During their adolescence in Aix, Paul Cézanne and Zola both bathed in the river Arc. It would never have crossed their minds to dive headfirst into the Bay of Marseilles. *Les Grandes Baigneuses* and *Les Baigneurs beside the Arc* would do likewise, preferring the coolness of fresh water and the shade of pine trees to the inhospitable rocks of the seashore. *Woman Diving into the Water* (1867–1870), was an exception. And when the painter silhouetted a young bather, arms crossed, on the shore, like *Le Grand Baigneur* and *Le Baigneur* (circa 1885), now in the Orsay Museum in Paris, it was in his imagination, designed to make the model a solitary effigy. The gaggle of bathers beside the river Arc had given way to an adolescent, melancholic giant, exiled on the bank like Cézanne himself during his stay at L'Estaque.

The neo-Impressionists painters who set up home in St. Tropez in the latter years of the 19th century did not attach much significance to the bather. Neither Signac nor Cross actually painted a Mediterranean swim. The young women beside the water in the great seaside compositions of neo-Impressionism borrowed more from the allegorical tradition of Puvis de Chavannes than from any description of scenes of life in a coastal resort, at that time still very embryonic in the Mediterranean. In his *Luxe, calme et volupté* (1904) and *Luxe I* and *II* (1907), Matisse likewise depicted a St. Tropez bay that was singularly devoid of bathers. It was not until Bonnard and the

130

On the raft at Monte Carlo Beach, 1934.
The sea, the nakedness, games in the water and in the sun, motionless time and that
"lightness of the earth above the sea, making you think of great departures and great landings"
that Pasolini found at the Riviera di Ponente, in the summer of 1959.

postwar years that see the Mediterranean beach filled with figures in bathing suits. The Bay of Cannes was then no longer just a set for allegorical naiads and water nymphs arriving from some imaginary *Doux Pays*, but a beach where golden figures caper about in the light of the setting sun. The mythological pretext might not have disappeared altogether from the picture as in *The Abduction of Europa*, but it nevertheless became muddled with the memory of a picnic on the Lérins Islands or a day in the coves. Bonnard's bather had conquered an existence which the neoclassical model would compete with for a long time to come. Picasso would never paint a Mediterranean bathing scene without thinking of placing it in a mythological universe. One of the last artists to make sacrifices to the genre, in order to mock it, was Picabia, who, on the Riviera liked nothing quite so much as those "flashy foreign" Venuses flanked by a large-nosed mask and those "piebald blacks," symbols of the age of fanatic sun worshippers. The wonderstruck visions of Lartigue could do nothing about it: the Mediterranean could not dodge the invasion of the beach; in no time at all, the paradise of Colette and Signac turned into an overcrowded territory which put Robinson to flight.

In *Swimming in the Sea*, Paul Morand sadly agreed: the Mediterranean had become the nightmare of the bather, an inferno of disfigured beaches, devoid of anything natural, and suffocated by a mutant crowd: "The Ligurian coast, as far as Genoa (that interminable Genoa)," he observed, "is so crowded, so crammed with buses and trucks (oh, the dark inner suburbs of Samperdarena!), so clogged with families packed onto its beach at Albaro, that you have to force on as far as Rapallo and Portofino to find a little nature." The litany of disenchantment with seaside resorts went on unabated. It clashed, as was well illustrated by Jean-Didier Urbain in *On the Beach*, with a "coastal dream," resisting apocalyptic visions with all its might.

Writers like Albert Camus embodied this triumph of the bather in pages that are still the most beautiful ever devoted to the joy of Mediterranean bathing. "I have to be naked and then plunge into the sea, still perfumed all over

[Above] Albert Camus at Leysin, 1947.
Who hasn't taken Noces suivi de l'Eté *with them, to read Camus in the Mediterranean?...*

[Facing] Alexandria, Egypt, 1998.
The boys of The Plague *in Cavafy's city. Diving head first into the blue, or the triumphant despair of the diver.*

with the essences of the land," we can read in *Marriages*, "washing these in those and putting around my skin the embrace for which earth and sea have pined for so long, lip to lip." Prior to 1936, few authors—and few painters—made the bather such a prototype of a "First Man" who, in the sea, undergoes the experience of a fullness and a rediscovered Mediterranean "pride." "Everywhere," wrote Camus, "people have often told me: there's nothing to be proud of. But yes, there is something: this sun, this sea, my heart bounding with youth, my body tasting of salt, and the vast setting where tenderness and glory meet in the yellow and the blue." Bathing is one of man's "marriages" with the world; it is also, as in *The Plague*, the only possible outlet offered to prisoners of the city: "For a few minutes, they advanced...solitary, far from the world, finally freed from the city and the plague." Liberating swims, glorious swims which, in the "baptism of salt," invent a veritable liturgy of happiness which is also the experience of a truth, "which is the truth of the sun and will also be the truth of my death."

But Camus did not manage to shed the ancient model any more than painters. In *Summer in Algiers*, the young men who bathe in the port are like "a wild cargo of gods," with links to the insolence and naïveté of the Greeks: "Today, and over and above this history, young people running on Mediterranean beaches is like the magnificent movements of the athletes of Delos." As an admirer of Nietzsche and Valéry, Camus did not, however, give in to the neoclassicism that dominated the 1930s; his bathers were not statues, but brown-skinned young men "stealing" a swim amid the red and black cargo ships of the Port of Algiers.

This sort of celebration does not recur in postwar literature—or if it does, it is only fleetingly. In *Les Petits Chevaux de Tarquinia*, published in 1953, Marguerite Duras describes the Italian holidays of two couples during a torrid summer. The sea in which the protagonists swam was anything but mythological: "The sea caused laughter." It might be simply "nice" or "beyond reproach," but it was never glorious. People swam in it because it was very hot; people sometimes dreamed of "sleeping in the sea," but without finding in it the repose which might heal boredom and love, or both at once. And the little Etruscan horses of Tarquinia wouldn't be any help this time, when it came to saving the summer from disaster.

For a writer like Erri De Luca, the experience of bathing in Ischia was something quite different. Swimming was a liberation, a sort of Icarus-like flight above the earth, unlike the vaguely Ophelian dreams of Gina in the Duras novel: "The sea," wrote De Luca, "gives the arms what the air offers wings, the swimmer floats above abysses. Upon my arrival in the early summer, I found myself naked. I broke loose from the earth that had held me for nine months in its rock and I swam by beating the sea water with my feathered feet and my winged arms, sitting on the rocks which were tree tops in the sea." The growing wildness of the bather can be read first of all on his skin: "Freedom consisted in thickening," he wrote, "covering oneself with a bark," otherwise put, becoming a landscape, and being now at one with the world. "If I am not a yellow layer of its cracked crust, split by the vines plunging into it, if thistles do not grow in my eyes, if I do not dream at night the way a rock dreams lulled by movements, it is because I shall never be able to learn." Today, this is still the daydream of the Mediterranean bather: to reinvent a morning of the world, to be one with the sea, and to learn once again how to live.

[Pages 134–135] *Les Calanques*, 1942–1944, Francis Picabia.
Among the images of happiness: the protective coves and inlets of the Mediterranean.

[Facing] *Children in the Sun*, 1907, Fernand Léger (detail).
Bathing in the Mediterranean: a "kind of mystical ceremony that has replaced religious worship,
but whose effectiveness in the spiritual domain has not yet been proven in any precise way."
(A. Bierce, quoted by Jean-Didier Urbain in On the Beach*).*

Figures

The Diva

The figure of the diva ("star" in Italian) left the shores of the Mediterranean several decades ago, and ended up in the larger sea of record companies. The heyday of the diva occurred in the 1950s with such singers as Maria Callas, born in Greece, Teresa Berganza, born in Spain, and the American Marilyn Horne. Since the 1920s, the movie star has often replaced her in the collective imagination. But the figure of the diva has kept her vocation as "superstar" intact. Her style is still that of the femme fatale with her mind-boggling metamorphoses—at times doleful and moaning, at times up in arms and indomitable; at times *mater dolorosa*, at times inaccessible goddess. Yet the diva, just like the age-old *Mamma*, is slipping away from us.

In the early 1970s, in Fellini's *Roma*, the director tried one last time to hold on to her. The scene has become a famous one. We are in Rome, on Via degli Astalli, in front of the Palazzo Altieri, with Anna Magnani walking towards it, followed by the camera. "Anna," says Fellini's voice, "what about saying a thing or two about Rome?" In front of the actress's impassive face, the voice-over keeps trying: "Look, Anna, you're almost a symbol of..." Magnani interrupts: "What d'you think I know?" and the voice-over goes on to define the Roman diva: "The she-wolf and the vestal virgin..." to which the star replies: "I don't want to know." Fellini takes up the thread: "How d'you think you're like Rome?" And it is then, before she shuts the heavy door of the Palazzo (this would be her final retort to the cinema), that Magnani says: "Go home (*Va a dormire Federi...*), I don't trust you."

The diva dismisses the filmmaker the way a mother dismisses her child or a woman betrayed dismisses a lover who she no longer trusts. In order to escape the part that the cinema wanted her to play one last time, the diva uses her arsenal. Actually, the actress embodied the two sides of the diva: madonna of the seven sorrows and goddess of refusal, brilliant actress and solitary figure. Anna Magnani played on both sides of her personality: cheeky, endowed with a hearty appetite for life, and wearing a tragic face; inseparably solemn and dazzling, as in the role which would, all on its own, earn her her fame: the widow Pina in Roberto Rossellini's *Roma, Città aperta* (1946).

The mother status is also the key to the character of Oum Kalsoum: *oum* meaning "mother" and *kalsoum*, the last child of the prophet: the chubby daughter. Oum Kalsoum assumed this twofold calling of the diva like no other singer: at once a "Lady" (*el Sett*) with her Pharaonic bearing and Scheherzade with her dizzying sensuality, "Star of the Orient" and peasant woman of the Nile. It was in this dual capacity that, from the 1930s onward, the Arab world overlapped with the ritual radio broadcasting, every first Thursday of the month, of a single new song by its idol. Oum Kalsoum first let a colossal orchestra strike up, prelude-like, sometimes making the audience wait more

138

Maria Callas.
All the roles, all the emotions, even beyond the voice, like Medea in Pasolini's film.

If Charles Maurras and Léon Daudet in *Our Provence* had wanted to see in Marseilles "the capital of the Mediterranean and not just the 'port of the Orient' as Puvis had put and painted it," they also added that it was, as well, "a very big village, shady, and filled with fish and seashells from top to bottom, familiar, welcoming, rakish in all likelihood and then some, but with cosy nooks, familiar and concentrated, passages with oaks and little donkeys, and shops from quite another time." The theme of plurality, of the Marseilles kaleidoscope, half village half megalopolis, still permeates the literature devoted to the city. But so does the theme of a happiness peculiar to Marseilles, which Stendhal described thus: "It was a simple happiness: a happiness of card games, games of *boules*, happiness of apéritifs and fishing sorties, family reunions and excursions with friends, happiness of little huts and boating, lotteries, in the cafés, in winter ...Happiness of café music and dancing, lunches of sea urchins...," happiness that Pagnol and much of the southern cinema would turn into some kind of stereotype.

If Marseilles offers the image of a Cubist city struggling to put its pieces back together, apart from

145

certain nights when there's a football match or a big popular festival in the Old Port. "Naples," in the words of Jean-Noël Schifano, "is the city of mergers." Whether you stray into its fabulous Baroque pastry shops, its funereal caves smelling of sulphur, its countless churches bedecked like reliquaries or one of its deafening markets, Naples is always at fever pitch. "Races, religions, philosophies, customs: like the four elements that merge in a staggering tectonic flow," Schifano continues, "tangible apocalypse, *Homo napolitanus* carries with him the cruel and fertile and fascinating outpourings of the ages: and his blood bears them along, vibrating from East to West, from Greece to Spain, from Christos to Osiris, from Priapos to Petrus; and from Homer to Virgil, Gesualdo to Scarlatti, Vico to Basile, Atellanes to Pulcinella, Tiber to Pedro of Toledo, tenth of the sixty viceroys, Ribera l'Espanolet to Gemito the Greek, from sirens' tombs to Aragonese princes' coffins, from the Sybilline trapezium at Cumae to obelisks—a single lava-flow where the children of Naples overwhelm, with their heavy flesh, their crazy laughter and their wings of fire."

Unlike Marseilles, Naples has managed to make the incredible diversity of its ingredients its own, play with its empty spaces and its quirky porousness, and its twisted settings where the Greek, Roman, Egyptian, Angevin, Norman and Spanish components of its buildings become entangled about one another, like *fumaruoli* of cocoa. Goethe was slightly disappointed to note that his quest, in Naples, for the stones of the city's origins still had a way to go. Naples lead the scholar astray. Everything about it was too eruptive, too liquid, too contrasting and too mixed at the same time, like the *sfogliatella* of Pintauro— a sweet volcano of fresh ricotta, cubes of candied marrow, zest of orange, vanilla and cinnamon, its sides the hue of honey. How to discover the original pasta in a city that boasts 83 varieties! How to describe a crowd, as Anna Maria Ortese does so well in *The Sea Does Not Lap at Naples*, which "moves like a snake smitten by the sun, but not yet slain"!

Curzio Malaparte could not have chosen a better moment for describing Naples, in *The Skin*, than that autumn of 1943, when the city rose up against the Germans while the Allied troops were landing at Paestum and Salerno. Naples, Malaparte tells his American friend Jack, who landed in the thick of the bombs exploding all over the Italy of Virgil and Horace, is "the most mysterious city in Europe, the only city in the ancient world that hasn't perished like Ilion, like Nineveh, like Babylon. It is the only city in the world that hasn't foundered in the huge collapse of the ancient civilization. Naples is a Pompeii that has never been buried. It is not a city, it is a world. The ancient, pre-Christian world, remains at the surface of the modern world." To add to the horrific depiction of the city prey to famine and the craziest agitation, Malaparte rounds off his Neapolitan ex-voto with the description of the eruption of Vesuvius which brings the chaos full circle. Among the most famous scenes of the narrative, what sticks is always this image of the terrified crowd, dashing into churches and squares, the faces and the façades of the houses bespattered by the dreadful glow of the volcano, "as in a photograph taken with magnesium," distraught soldiers and the celebration that follows the first lull with cries of *è fortuna! è fortuna!*

148

Everything about this flow of death and crazed uprising contrasts with the portrait of Venice. "Venice was born out of nothing, from a bit of mud and the foam of the sea, like Venus, her almost-homonym," wrote Philippe Braunstein and Robert Delort in the book they dedicated to that city. But the image we create of it for ourselves is made up of a series of Venices: "You like the Piazzetta," wrote Fernand Braudel, "Marcel Proust, who merely paid Venice a brief visit, liked it too. You like the Zattere opposite the only real sea river (the Giudecca canal) that flows to Mestre... but John Ruskin also adored the Zattere." You're invariably following somebody in Venice. This might well be the explanation behind the little scenario that Sophie Calle perfected in her *Suite vénitienne*, attracting the following comment from Baudrillard: "The city is built like a trap, a maze, a labyrinth that inevitably and inexorably and as if stealthily leads people back to the same points, by way of the same bridges, across the same squares, along the same quays and wharves. Everyone is following everyone else in Venice, through force of circumstance, everyone meets everyone else, and everyone recognizes everyone else. Better still: the only way of not meeting somebody in Venice is to follow him or her at a distance and never lose sight of them." In order not to miss out on the encounter and to avoid the risk of being followed, Venetians discovered the magic parade by wearing masks for almost six months a year. All this required was a mask with a white, sharp-beaked bird, attached to the *bautta*, a black cloak covering the shoulders surmounted by a hood and a tricorne cocked hat, and the large *tabarro*, the black domino that disguised the silhouette. Secret agents and other professional informants tracking people day and night in Casanova's Venice, saw their task complicated by the fact that Sior Maschera was here, there and everywhere: in the courts, at mass, in the market, in the café, in the visiting rooms of monasteries, in the Palazzo, in the dives and gaming houses and brothels; everywhere that going incognito protected people from snitches. One does not hide in Venice to die, as Barres and Thomas Mann thought, but out of happiness, with a soft spot for the parties and pleasures that then made La Serenissima the capital of an "unimaginable panic," as President De Brosses observed.

Like Marseilles, Istanbul offers its visitors several cities rolled into one. It is vast, and initially discouraging because of the kind of dusty frenzy that grips it, because of its crazy traffic and pollution, rivaling Mexico City. In winter, the clouds of lignite covering it exhale a cellar-like smell, close to explosion. People don't really know if the city is getting ready to be ravaged by fire again, as happened when all the buildings were wooden, or whether its thousands of trucks hurtling along like flying fortresses will eventually leave it to be gently buried beneath the earthquake that is endlessly tormenting it. In *The Black Book*, Ohran Pamuk opted for the Bosphorus, with its undoubted archaeological properties, drying up. But for Ahmet Hamdi Tanpïnar, author of *Five Cities*, Istanbul is also the most beautiful introduction to the cities of Turkey, "the city of cool, limpid, beneficial springs. In exactly the same way as it was for [his] father the city with the most splendid mosques, the city of minstrels and

muezzins with their lovely voices." Sources to which the Turkish language has given names with "sparkling consonants," meaning "the little spring," "healing water," "the gold embroideress"... Have the fountains described by Tanpïnar suffered the same fate as the muezzins, who have now been replaced by wailing loudspeakers? It could well be so...

As the principal destination on the Oriental journey, Constantinople gave rise to such a prolific literature that passing writers gave up describing the city from the end of the 18th century onward. Most of the visitors who went there in the 19th century spread the poetic vision of a world where the picturesque is king. But unlike what happened with Venice, Potocki, Lamartine, Nerval, Gautier, the Countess of Barbarin and Loti would not make Istanbul a city that you visit in the footsteps of a beloved author. The city they described has been engulfed in the megalopolis of more than twelve million inhabitants that came into being in the 1960s. And there is no certainty that the city of Tanpïnar, with its strange neighborhoods, will withstand the cataclysm much longer. "While you are in Istanbul," wrote the author of *Five Cities*, "going about your business, you feel a desire to be in Nichantachï, and when you are in Nichantachï, it is Eyüp and Usküdar that you want to see when all your business is done..." These sudden desires to escape, explains Tanpïnar, "are fueled by the beauty of nature, works of art, lifestyles and a host of reminiscences."

[Page 150] Old Nice.

[Page 151] *View of Marseilles*, circa 1955, Nicolas de Staël.
"Nice the beautiful" and "the Athens of the Gauls": two contrasting fates,
which both suffer equally from their poor image.

[Facing] Rambla in downtown Barcelona with the Lyceum theatre.
A Mediterranean model of the urban art of living at the hour of the paseo,
the equivalent of the passegiata *in Italy and the* promenade à serein *in France.*

Squares

"I suffocated in Rome and Florence—suffocated in awe—," wrote Julien Gracq in that odd breviary of the thwarted traveller called *Around the Seven Hills*, "a bit like within the confines of a windowless museum: aesthetic ferment in a closed vessel, excess in the cramming of art associated with a lack of room and distances." The only outlet for this surplus of school memories and remote-controlled admiration: the public place. There, monuments are less important than the delicious void hewn out of the dense layers of the city.

Actually, what saves people walking round Rome from asphyxiation is those "squares, big and little, which no major road leads to, where you unexpectedly find yourself as if in the central area of a labyrinth." Unlike the masterpiece you head for in a procession of people, the square materializes without warning; it is an unexpected gift. "The urban fairyland," wrote Gracq, "is linked more than once, for the solitary stroller, with those protected crannies, whose unforeseen access is less like the use of a general convenience than like a private favor." But it's important that the square isn't invaded by the throng of "extras" that the visitor encounters everywhere on his rounds. How beautiful the Piazza Navona is when the "pastry-cutter design that forms its even, stadium-like oval in the very midst of a compact mass of buildings" isn't spoiled by huddles of tourists sitting on the Tre Scalini terrace sampling that incomparable *tartufo*! And how magnificent the Piazza di Spagna would be, "arraying on its steps hippies from every country in Europe," were it not that "altar of repose for the sunny tiredness of living, a set for the flower vendor of Limelight, for a sweet and sentimental adventure upon which the Church of the Trinità dei Monti rains down from on high its soothing religiosity, the curfew of its quaint angelers bells."

The city Julien Gracq dreamed of resembles De Chirico's paintings of squares: deserted, illuminated by a "marvelous light" which Nietzsche had found in Turin, with its "stark and solemn squares" where "the arcades seem to meet a need." It is an ideal city, straight out of the models for history books and epics; a city so perfectly imagined that a visit to it can only be a disappointment. Proust in Venice glimpsed by night one of those "vast and sumptuous campos," which he tried to find again next day. He never managed to, just like Julien Gracq, seeking, beneath the cultural alluvia covering Rome, the aerial ideal city in his mind's eye. Yet many Italian squares are designed like theatrical apparitions—thus we find the Piazza del Campo in Siena, the Piazza Ducale in Vigevano, and the Trevi Fountain across which, one night in *La Dolce Vita*, Anita Ekburg walked as if in those naval battles that, in the month of August, used to turn the Piazza Navona into a watery arena. What would Julien Gracq have thought of Siena's Piazza del Campo on the day of the Palio, or Venice's Piazza San Marco during the carnival?

154

Square in Siena, Tuscany, Italy.
*The Piazza del Campo in Siena, in the shadow of the Palazzo Pubblico and the Torre del Mangia,
a shell of pink bricks erected on the "field" and turned to the sky, divided into nine segments.
Heart of the palio, navel of a square, the city's umbilicus.*

Mediterranean squares are not merely "decorative squares," as Quatremère de Quincy wrote about San Marco, but places where the city and a whole region put themselves on view. What square could symbolize this more than the Jamaa el-Fna square in Marrakech, which Edith Wharton observed in her book *In Morocco* that it was "the center of all the life, all the distractions and all the tittle-tattle of Marrakech"? Architecture, here, plays no role, save for the silhouette of the Koutoubia in the setting sun, seen from the terraces of the Café de France. The old esplanade of the Anéantissement [Devastation or Annihilation]—also known as the Square of Destruction and the Square of the Departed, where people were hanged in droves, which was also called the Square of Traffic when it was the meeting place of caravans coming from Demnat, Tameslout, Moulouya, Souss and the ports on the Atlantic and the Mediterranean, as well as the Mosque of Ruination, the Gathering of Nobodies, the Square of Nothingness...—offers a non stop spectacle. It is a phantasmagoria that depends on more than the flickering,

156

The Flagellation of Christ, after 1444, Piero della Francesca.
The Italian square is a metaphysical space: between a stage for execution or torture, extreme mellowness, deafening parade and code of silence.

smoky glow of the scene it ceaselessly offers, from group to group: snake charmers, storytellers, singers, transvestite dancers, Gnawoua musicians, acrobats from Amizmiz, monkey-trainers, medicine-men and healers, soothsayers and jugglers. Aïssouas with shaven heads, echoing, as part of the spectacle, the countless merchants described by Jérôme and Jean Tharaud in *Marrakech or the Lords of the Atlas*, drawing up a listing that still holds good: "Merchants of anything and everything, green barley, limestones, wood and cut straw; merchants of oranges, lemons, pomegranates..., vendors of cotton fabrics, secondhand clothes dealers and bric-à-brac traders,...mattress makers, cobblers...vendors of cooked grasshoppers, hard-boiled eggs sprinkled with cumin, chick-peas, grilled beans; soup merchants squatting in front of a huge pot surrounded by greasy cloths; merchants of weird concoctions made of sugar, almonds, dates, grapes and millet seed; ironmongers sitting in front of cat skins, owl and sparrow-hawk wings, remains of dried creatures, lizards, chameleons and so on."

157

[Above] *Roman Square*, 1921, Giorgio de Chirico.

[Pages 158–159] *Gli Italiani si voltano*, Milan, 1954, Mario de Biasi.
The piazza, an outdoor living-room where the stage of desire is boundless.

Places

Cafés

There is no better spot to take in passing beauty than the Mediterranean café. In his *Little Guide for Cities With No Past*, written just after the war, Albert Camus drew up a list for Algeria of yesteryear: "The terrace of the Café des Facultés, on rue Michelet in Algiers, provided that you are there on a Sunday morning in the month of April... In Oran, the Cintra bar on the Boulevard Gallieni is also a good observatory. In Constantine, you can always stroll around the music stand... I recommend to the sensitive traveller, who happens to be in Algiers, to go and drink an anisette or two under the arches in the port..." What has become of Camus' bars? What places do the young people of Algiers gravitate to these days after the beach? Does the youth of Alexandria still hang out in the same bistros around the port? Are the Pastroudis of Cavafy, Tsirkas, Ungaretti and Lawrence Durrell still around? And what about the San Stephano, the Café Mahfouz as Daniel Rondeau calls it, because the writer was a regular customer there? And the countless Lacarrière cafés in Greece? And the famed El-Fichaoui in Cairo near El-Azbar? Are the Négresco in Tangiers, where the author of *Naked Bread* wrote the chapters of the novels that he then submitted little by little to Paul Bowles, and the Roxy still open? And what about the dilapidated cafés where the Beat generation hung out? And the Moorish café on the way to the mercantile district after the Forbes palace, reached by a dirt track leading up to a small gate smothered in bougainvillea, opening on to shady terraces, lined with mats, where you could spend hours and hours drinking mint tea and smoking grass looking out on to the Strait of Gibraltar, at once colossal and minute, with its ships plying to and fro and its shoals of fish like metallic gusts on the water's surface—what's happened to that place, too?

The Mediterranean is a land of outdoor cafés and terraces. Some, with no special fanfare, subscribe to the religion of happiness and contentment, others are awash with tourists. Like museums of time passing, they display the list of their illustrious dead who one day came to sip their espresso for ever and a day. It's impossible to walk along Via dei Condotti without stopping outside that ordinary, plush Roman café, the café Greco, which mixes the scent of cappuccino with the savory aromas of the morning's pastries. It is here, since 1760, that Goethe, Gogol, Mendelssohn, Stendhal, Baudelaire, Wagner and hordes of celebrities have ventured to inhale the same savory, sweet smell. How can you settle down on the terrace of the café Rosati on the Piazza del Popolo without telling yourself, as you crumple one of its wonderful paper napkins with its Art déco design: "I'm at the Rosati," where so many writers, artists and politicians have come before me,

160

Square of the Forum in Arles, 1888, Vincent Van Gogh.
Places where the Mediterranean promenader comes to sniff, he knows not quite why, the beauty of drama and tragedy in the pure state, or the dazzle of a star-studded sky above the "high yellow note" of the Van Gogh picture.

while the din of the traffic, just a few steps away, should really be prompting me to more gloomy considerations? You might well prefer the discreet café on the Piazza Santo Eustachio, behind the Sapienza, where you will sample the purest espresso in all Rome, or perhaps a nameless café in the old ghetto, so cramped that there's hardly room to stand between the gleaming counter and the magic mirror, just long enough to down a scorching hot coffee with licorice.

People have also extolled Venetian cafés other than the Quadri and the Florian, which are no longer frequented by the "long moustaches with their confident weariness" dear to Paul Morand, and Harry's Bar, which, as the author of *Venices* points out for us, was opened in 1920 "before Orson Welles and Hemingway." Here, still, you may drink your Bellini surrounded by Americans or prefer the bars of the Dorsoduro, the Campo Santo Stefano and the Campo Santa Margherita at passeggiata hour, or alternatively, at about seven in the evening, with the Venetians, you may head for the Piazza della Merceria, not far from the Rialto, turned into an outdoor café popular with a throng of locals and regulars.

What greater pleasure than to stroll round the streets of Seville looking for your first *cafe con leche* (the lightest, which is oddly called *sombra*), matched at the other end of the day by the last *cafe solo* in the Barrio Santa Cruz, around the cathedral, or at Triana in the Calle Betis? What would Lisbon be without Pessoa, and the Brasileira on the Rua Garrett, outside which the writer now has his statue in the form of a bar pillar, Lisbon without its *fin de siècle* cafés towards Don Pedro IV square? The traveller touring these Mediterranean cafés should make a stop at the Nicola or the Pastelaria Suiça in Barcelona; he would certainly take us to the Café de l'Opéra on La Rambla dels Caputxins or the very chic Dos Torres, on the via Augusta, from where, as from the Zürich, on the Plaza de Catalunya, you can watch Barcelona's youth. But here, too, the cafés you go into, book or paper in hand, have something more to them than those in guidebooks, and will lure you to unlikely discoveries. Is the Bar Club, of which Juan Goytisolo was so fond, still there? And what about the Echouage, with its tables arranged on a pontoon floating amid "coils of rope, trawl lines and stanchions from wrecks": has it withstood the changes that have happened in Barceloneta, which has turned into the city's sculpture promenade? And what of the *Ikbal* ("Happiness") in Istanbul, hard by the Nuruosmaniye mosque, where Turkish writers used to meet fifty years ago? Nor could you stay in Istanbul without doing as Nerval and Gautier did, and partaking of the rite of the *kahvehâne*, a 16th-century Yemeni invention, legend has it, with which the Sufi sect accompanied its ceremonies, regardless of the *fatwas* that decreed it a drug.

When Jean de Thévenot went to Syria in the 16th century, he noticed that "all the cafés of Damascus are magnificent, they are refreshing and pleasing places." Yet most of the cafés, as pointed out by Alexandre Hepp in his *Minutes d'Orient*, had "neither gold nor dark red velvet, but almost at every step a low shop with whitewashed walls, a mat on the ground, an oven, a round divan, gaudy and sagging..." The traveller was usually surprised by the bareness of these places, with their occasional decorations vainly trying to

164

[Page 162] Palestina, 1999, Jean Marc Tingaud

[Page 163] Lounge of a hotel in Agadir before the earthquake.
The Mediterranean café: a snapshot of life in the sun which survives the caricature of Marius.

embellish them. He also had a premonition about the seedy place designed to hoodwink him or drag him towards some "wan debauchery." Some of these cafés also offered the services of a barber and a reading room. Others were renowned for the perjurers who could be enlisted from them with a nod of recognition. In Istanbul, in the boilermakers' neighborhood, Nerval heard "wonderful tales recited and declaimed by professional storytellers associated with Stamboul's leading cafés," who, in the manner of rhapsodists, embroidered the thousand and one versions of the story of Solomon and the Queen of Sheba. Théophile Gautier, who liked "having one of those little cups of cloudy coffee there, brought to you by an odd young man with large dark eyes, poised on his fingertips, in a large eggcup of silver filigree or pierced copper," would be surprised by the presence of "all sorts of prints and engravings of the most baroque taste and choice, which in no way seem to shock Muslim orthodoxy." Ahmet Hamdi Tanpïnar describes them "with their ponds, fountains, Turkish pipes with amber mouthpieces arrayed along the walls, their broad windows sometimes giving on to the loveliest landscapes of the city, the old Turkish cafés whose ceilings and paneling, shutters and finely worked canopies have been so extolled by travellers. In these cafés," Tanpïnar continues, "frequented, depending on the district, by members of the middle class, craftsmen, Turkish soldiers, or alternatively, when they were located by the sea, fishermen and boatmen, there were storytellers recounting tales and *saz* players (a long-necked stringed instrument) who took part in poetic tournaments."

Then, in 1839, came the *Tanzimat* (the "reorganization") which put an end to the café that was such a part of those Oriental journeys. The old divans were replaced by the tables, chairs and ice creams of European cafés. The Piyer Loti café in Eyüp, on the Golden Horn, is an Orientalist café, while towards Beyoghlu and Taksim, and the modern neighborhoods of Istanbul, the fashion is for the grand café of Paris and Vienna. The Mediterranean cafés that one imagined to be as changeless as the sea are caught up in the age of summer fashions and crazes.

Medinas

Nineteenth-century guidebooks condescendingly called it the "native city" or "native town," anarchic, disreputable and seedy, to compare it with the clear and organized "European city" or "European town," which Lyautey had built outside, true to his "theory of separateness." In the 1950s, the medina still referred to the traditional Muslim town or city with its customary batch of disparaging clichés.

In *Au Maroc*, Pierre Loti turns out to be by far the most critical commentator. "Old Fez" for him was just "one long sinister street, between high walls all cracked and blackish, with no window to brighten them up..., a maze of dark, covered streets, crisscrossing in all directions..." Its gardens, few and far between, were "extremely sad." The predominant impression was one of "dead old age." Everywhere he looked he saw the same sight of desolation: "The walls are worn, gnawed by lichen...the houses are crumbling and awry...the stones have no corners any more." The wretched and overwhelmed visitor, afflicted by homesickness, roamed amid a nameless labyrinth: "It's as if you were walking at the bottom of a series of wells adjoining one another by means of arches: you only get brief glimpses of the blue or grey of the sky, and it's impossible to get your bearings in the inextricable maze."

In their book *Marrakech or the Lords of the Atlas*, Jérôme and Jean Tharaud describe the Red City in similar terms, as "an inextricable maze of lanes, dead-ends, long vaulted passages, endlessly ramified, getting lost like so many roots in the confused mass of houses." The medina was a shapeless heap of half-abandoned houses where the visitor was forever coming up against "fallen blocks" and "mysterious gates and doors, and you never know whether they're going to open on to a palace, a hovel, a stable or some saint's tomb..."

Henri Bosco, in his book *From Sand to Sea*, described Fez as one of those "cities which merely offer the eye enigmas and, on closer investigation, just walls, or inextricable labyrinths. Cities with folds and creases and complications, where there is no wall, door, gate, byway or human shadow that ... doesn't disconcert and at times alarm by their inextricable nooks and crannies, and their routes which don't lead anywhere."

Its inhabitants were not housed in the best of conditions. In 1955, the author of *Casablanca, City of Riots*, M. de La Varde, devoted to the medina a hateful pamphlet written by a settler on the point of leaving: "A medieval city in the middle of Chicago, with sordid, narrow lanes, full of potholes, terraced houses sloppily whitewashed, hundreds of tiny, disused mosques, with a seething, filthy populace, picturesque people call it, a racial cocktail gabbling away in Mediterranean tongues—Arabs, Berbers, Sephardic Jews,

Moulay Idriss Street in Fez.
*The medina: neither the capital (*qasaba*), nor the metropolis (*misr*),
not even a mere town (*balad*), but the "supreme city," like certain old towns of the Midi.*

Spaniards, Frenchmen and European half-castes. It's Smyrna [Izmir], it's Gallipoli, it's Thessalonika, it's one of the mediocrely Mediterranean aspects that would not be disavowed by Panaït Istrati, it's Casa before the conquest, before Lyautey, whose history Istiqal lays claim to, smelling olives in their brine, fried fish, mutton kebabs, prickly pears and piss."

Since then, the medina has been turned into an "historic center"; tourist guides invite you to wander at will in it, recommending that you literally lose your way so that its spell will work that much better on you, describing in every detail its architectural wealth and extolling its souk or bazaar. "The exploration of souks," notes the Blue Guide about Marrakech, "is a wonderful adventure and calls for complete abandon and availability." Since 1981, Fez has been part of the "World Heritage" list of cities, swiftly followed by Marrakech in 1985 and Meknes in 1990. Impressive renovation work has been undertaken in all three, and music festivals have been organized. In these ancient cities, those who are mad about traditional houses purchase a *dâr* or a *riad*, which they painstakingly restore, and then publish pictures of their new residence in books about the art of living in Morocco (we thus find the Strasser, Naouar, Sabbane, Maïté, Nougoum and Suleyman *dârs* in Marrakech). More restaurants, galleries and antique shops open each year, enticing foreigners into the once protected and sacred space of the city.

The image of the medina has actually changed; it is no longer the inextricable disorder described by bygone travellers, but an ideal place for finding shelter and a roof over your head; and what is more paradoxical still, it represents a threatened order which must these days be respected and protected. An extended visit to a medina brings forth, from the apparent disorder, a coherent urban system that alters our points of reference, our landmarks and our perception of space. The medina thus appears through its sequence of thresholds: the threshold of the house set staggered in such a way as to protect the privacy of the place, the threshold of the inner courtyard or *west ed-dâr*, off which radiate the apartments, and the threshold of the terrace that acts as the roof. The neighborhood where the house is situated, the *hayy* or the *derb*, connects by way of a gate or door, the *bab*, which used to be shut at night in the dead-end alleys of the *derb*, the busy street at the end, with its shops and stores, the hammam, the Koranic school and places of prayer. The main street or thoroughfare, the *chawari*, used by foreigners and strangers, leads from one city gate to the next, by way of the great mosque and the mercantile center, which is itself separated from the residential suburbs by the city walls and the no-man's-land, the *cheikla*. This topography soon becomes part of the way we get our bearings, it guides us more surely than any city map, and it gives us the sensation of venturing into a world that is turning at our pace. "If we compare the city to an organism," wrote Walter M. Weiss in *Bazaar: Markets and Merchants of the Islamic World*, "and its network of streets to the circulatory system, the houses are the lung cavities, the *harat* play the part of capillary vessels, the *chawari* that of the arteries and main veins. The aortas help people to make for the city gates in one direction, and the bazaar—the heart of the city—in the other."

[Page 168] The medina in Tetouan, Morocco, Jean Marc Tingaud.
The gates: a threshold in the series of walls that protect the medina.

[Page 169] *The Gate of the Casbah*, 1912, Henri Matisse.

[Facing] Bazaar in Constantinople, Félix Ziem.
From Pierre Loti to Paul Bowles by way of Jacques Berque and Juan Goytisolo, all those writers who have been intrigued by the Arab city have described the beauty of the medina, daily explored its maze of light and shadow, delved into its scorching lanes, without ever covering the distance that separates the intruder from the real city.

Markets

One morning in the month of July 1755, Giacomo Casanova, who, as was his wont, had spent the night in some gaming-room or chamber of love, was returning to his quarters by way of the Erberia, which looks across to the Fondaco dei Tedeschi, right next to the Rialto. The aisles of the covered market had not yet been invaded by the throng. It felt nice walking before the day's great heat, and Casanova often lingered hereabouts. He was not the only one. And what's more, as he would point out in his *History of My Life*: "It is not true that young people go to the Erberia before sunrise to enjoy that pleasure [the cool of early day]; it's just a pretext for them. The people who go there are the amorous and gallant men and women who have spent the night in the casinos and inns, and in the frenzy of gambling...The men who go there with women are keen to rouse the envy of their peers by displaying their good fortune. Those who go there all on their own are seeking to make discoveries or stir up jealousies; and the women go there more to be seen than to see. They are very pleased that everyone realizes that they are not embarrassed. Flirtation and coquetry are out of the question because of the raggedy aspect of their finery. On the contrary, it seems that the women are eager to show themselves in that particular place in all that disorder and that they want those who see them there to think carefully about it."

But why the market? Was it because of its closeness to the bridge, over which Venetians had to pass, or its roof on rainy days? Or was it because of the life you were bound to find there from dawn onward? Or again was it because of that particular freedom that outdoor markets enjoy, which makes your step quicken, with greater briskness and abandon than elsewhere? On account of this morning procession of untidy beauties, among the vegetables and herbs of Friuli, the Erberia will always be the most Venetian of markets. There are others, near the church of San Pantaleon, which books about Venice single out, because you can buy your wares there directly from the quayside, from boats laden with shiny vegetables, beneath pale cloth awnings. But these floating shops do not a market make. What they lack is the din and disordered finery.

It's true that Mediterranean markets are not just places where you do your shopping. Their spirit is a mixture of a wide range of pretexts. The local person who does his business there also goes there to see what's happening and talk about the state of the world. The tourist stocks up on colors, cries, smells, unknown products and exotic labels. This is where the politician presses his constituents' flesh. It is here, say the historians, that popular uprisings and revolutions are sparked. Some people have been predicting the death of the market since the 1960s with the spread of supermarkets and shopping malls. The risk of seeing them vanish is no longer so great these

172

Market in Marrakech, Jean Marc Tingaud.
*Livestock market in Morocco and Egypt, Mediterranean fish markets, the truffle market at Alba,
the covered San Lorenzo market in Florence, the Verona market on the Piazza delle Erbe, the markets
at Uzès and Palermo: the Mediterranean of markets: a geography of spices, perfumes, cries and colors.*

days, but another threat is hanging over them—the danger that they will become just another tourist attraction. All we'll have to do, though, is avoid the rush hour and start when Casanova used to start, with a tour of the market, like the hero created by André Pieyre de Mandiargues in *The Edge*, in Barcelona, who, "intrigued by girls who were usually brown-skinned and dark-haired, extending upwards by a white jug perched on their heads," let himself be drawn to the market of San José: "One dark Isis seemed to order him to follow her between the white vegetable stands, overflowing with red peppers and tomatoes. Another, no less solemn, drew him into the fish hall, where she deserted him among great crayfish with their sorrowful drooping antennae, large prawns, *carabinieri* of a purple hue more intense in the raw state than after being cooked, octopuses, cuttlefish and squid dappled like ocelots. Red mullet, scorpion fish and pink bream make him think, without him really knowing why, of grapes and tigers, as if they had been brought together in a slimy heap to be borne along by some Dionysian procession." Not all Mediterranean markets have this dreamlike dignity, but Pieyre de Mandiargues understood it: the most beautiful markets are those protected by favorable gods, ready to take you by the hand, and abandon you between the monster's claws.

The Campo dei Fiori in Rome has nothing extraordinary about it; it's one of those countless Italian markets that takes over a square. But here, the sombre statue of Giordano Bruno, who was burnt alive in 1600 on the orders of Pope Urban VIII for having given his backing to Copernicus' heliocentric theories, contributes the tragic color that suits the displays of fennel root, peppers, aubergines, purple artichokes, curly Treviso chicory, cardoons

174

[Above] Sheep market in Egypt.

[Facing] Fish market in Provence.
Be it a forum for trade or a tourist destination, the market is also one of the last settings of the Mediterranean lifestyle.

and little bunches of herbs. Something sacred and slightly frightening must also reign over the market of Trajan in Rome, with its five floors and its 500 *tabernae* (stands and shops): flowers on the ground floor, wine and oil on the first, spices on the second and third, the administration on the fourth, and fish on the fifth and last. The huge construction built by Apollodorus of Damascus was an attempt to bring order to Rome's markets, whose incredible chaos and deafening din had been railed against by both Juvenal and Martial. But these markets put up resistance to the "large surfaces" of Trajan's. And for a long time Rome still looked like an open air market. The image of the Mediterranean market has nevertheless been permanently altered. Its dead straight plan started to resemble that of a city within a city, with its reserved positions and its pipes and channels. Often, as at San Lorenzo in Florence, and beneath the lofty plane trees of the Place aux Herbes in Aix-en-Provence, the arrangement of the stalls reminds us of that ancient ordering of things.

It is this architecture of Roman markets that we also think of when we venture into the great bazaars of Istanbul and Cairo. As in Rome, the covered market there looks like a city within a city, "with its streets," observed Théophile Gautier in his *Constantinople* (1853), "its lanes and back streets, its passages and alleys, its crossroads, its squares, its fountains, an inextricable labyrinth where you have trouble finding your way around, even after several visits." So the bazaar was an inevitable feature of travel literature, and still is, even if it is coming up against competition from the souk, synonym of disorder and noise, which traps you in its maze of shops, workshops and cheap eateries, to the point of suffocation.

175

Mosques

The mosque sits at the heart of the Muslim world, in the midst of the shops of the bazaar, not far from the hammam, adjoining the local school, on the tourist track; its door opens on to the street like any shop door; you might think it just a place of passage, another threshold among many others—merely a little more unadorned and a little more open.

The Koran actually does make it a simple passage (a *bazakh*) between the secular and the spiritual. The mosque is a place of gathering (*al-djâmi*). There is nothing church- or temple-like about it, it isn't a place apart, isolated from other places by being especially hallowed; its place is inside the city, in the dense fabric of houses and shops, well within reach of sandals, rugs and fruit stands. "The mosque," wrote Ulya Vogt-Göknil in his book about the great mosques of Islam, "is not a sanctuary, in the pagan or perhaps Buddhist sense of the term; it is not the house of God, in the Christian sense, in other words the place where God himself is present," but a simple oratory. It is the place where you venerate God, where you kneel down after cleansing yourself, where you touch the ground with your forehead pointing in the direction of Mecca—after having also been the place where community issues used to be thrashed out.

The model for the mosque is the house that the prophet had built, lending a hand himself, after his departure for Medina in 622: "To the north," recounts Gabriele Crespi in *The Arabs in Europe*, "he built a kind of large room covered by a roof made of mud and palm fronds; the rear wall was oriented towards Jerusalem. To the east he had two small rustic houses built for Samda and Aisha, the two spouses of the Envoy of Allah after the death of his first wife, Khadija. On the southwest side stood a refuge for the poor. All the rooms gave on to the courtyard. Thus came into being, in that small town which was subsequently known as Madinat-al Nabi [Medina, "the city of the Prophet"], the first mosque, and one of the lowliest, which Muhammad refused to alter or improve, for "a building is the vainest of undertakings which may devour the wealth of a believer."

So its basic plan may be summed up as follows: a rectangular courtyard (*sahn*) turned towards the Kaaba, with, at its centre, a pool for ablutions (*midha*). The gallery (*mujâta*) that runs along the courtyard sometimes boasts the dimensions of a large loggia punctuated by columns. The imam, or prayer leader, stands in a niche called the *mihrâb*. The *minbâr*, which is one of the rare pieces of furniture within the mosque, looks like a small portable ladder, and acts as the seat for the preacher; the one belonging to Muhammad was a smallish seat of tamarisk wood made by a Byzantine Coptic craftsman. Since those early

176

Istanbul, Turkey, 1996.
*You'll either love it or hate it, the guidebooks warn. Istanbul is the city of every kind of frontier.
Sometimes Asian, sometimes western, half-village half-megalopolis; extreme chill and intense heat,
ruins and buildings are pitted against one another in a relentless duel.*

days, all sorts of *minbârs*, incorporated in the mosque's actual architecture, have been made. The floor, which used to be bare earth in bygone times, is covered with carpets these days, and the mosque itself is lit by chandeliers varying greatly in size and with differing degrees of elaborateness, ranging from the gigantic wheels of Istanbul's mosques to the most modest of light bulbs. The minaret (*midhâna*), which rises up above the central courtyard in the symbolic extension of the *mihrâb*, on the side opposite the prayer hall, is often the only sign whereby you can recognize the mosque; from it, the muezzin or crier proclaims the call to worship fives times a day. Everything within the mosque must be designed on the basis of an equality of the axes and cardinal points, as well as—as some would put it—the horizontals and verticals, as if an effort were being made to do away with what might bound the space, and represent it for itself. Anyone who has visited the Great Mosque in Cordoba will not fail to have been struck by this mirror-like repetition of the same columns and the same arches in what resembles an endless forest.

To better stress the immensity of Islam, and the dimension of infinity that the smallest of mosques is meant to suggest through its spare starkness, Muhammad declared: "The throne of God is on the water." Was it in response to this idea, as seems to be suggested by Baltasar Porcel in his *Mediterranean*, that King Hassan II had built beside the ocean in Casablanca one of the most impressive modern mosques in the Islamic world? In it, you can certainly see the image of a lighthouse—modern Islam built as if going out to meet the New World. Based on the same model, geometric motifs and carpets create more or less endless layers, like boundless expanses where the spirit will not come upon any obstacles, oriented as it is towards Mecca. For only the Kaaba is marked, it alone features a center (once Jerusalem, where "the distant mosque" is located, had been relegated to the background), a "Holy of Holies," whose boundaries may be emphasized, and measurements consecrated: a cube measuring ten metres by twelve, and sixteen metres in height. Yet the Kaaba does not house any holy writing or any relic, but "the curtain of divine Mercy" (the *rûhman*), which shrouds the elusive center of the soul. Draped in the black velvet *kismâ* embroidered with inscriptions in gold, it must not appear in its naked form to the pilgrim: its sacredness is hidden from view, beyond any kind of grasp; the pilgrim never gazes upon it head-on, but from the side, as he walks ceaselessly around it. Thus out of sight, the Kaaba cannot be turned into an object of idolatry. Needless to say, no image may take its place either, the Prophet having declared: "O ye who believe! Wine, games of chance, dressed stones and divinatory arrows are an abomination and a work of the Devil! Shun them... Perhaps you will be happy." A *sunna* relating the deeds and words of the Prophet specifies: "The angels do not go into a temple where there are images, bells and dogs." And adds, like a threat: "On the day of the Resurrection, the most fearsome punishment will be inflicted upon the painter who has imitated beings created by God, who will then say: 'Give life to these creations.'" Because the founder of a sect by the name of Abu Amir had broken this rule, he saw his mosque destroyed by Muhammad. It was called, to set an example, "the mosque of nuisance." Yet the mosque must also be a place dedicated to beauty.

180

On a journey to Istanbul, Lamartine was wonderstruck by the skill of Sinan, Suleyman's architect: "You feel that Muhammadism had its very own art, its ready-made art, in accordance with the radiant simplicity of its idea, when it erected these simple, regular, splendid temples, with no shadows shrouding its mysteries, and no altars for its victims." Its most famous examples are also masterpieces like the Dome of the Rock in Jerusalem, the Great Mosques of Damascus, Cairo, Baghdad and Kairouan. In any event, the work of the architect and ornamentalist must call divine oneness to mind, and relate back to the dimension which is the dimension of the Whole, which the mosque is merely a reminder of, jogging the memory. In its job as memory (the *dhikr*), it is accompanied by the psalmody of the muezzin and calligraphy that, along with geometry, must celebrate the infinite sphere of influence of the divine essence. Whence this amazement on the part of many a visitor in a place that lays such powerful claim to belonging to an indivisible totality, and its incorporation within the most cramped of medinas.

There is an element which both tangibly and symbolically represents this movement between the city and the mosque, and it is water. The water required for ablutions, its presence at times scaled down to bare essentials, with a simple tap in a wall and its rivulet to drain the used water away, or alternatively assuming the form of an architectural object in its own right, as in the Suleymaniye in Istanbul. The city is gathered around the mosque the way it gathers around a watering point. Close by, baths, souks and bazaars can all thrive. Its cool freshness, enhanced by the green hues of wall ceramics, suggests the idea of a flower-strewn garden. In it, it is as if you can breathe a little fresh air in the heat of the afternoon, during a siesta, or alternatively you may see it as an uncluttered place where life can reassume its rightful qualities.

Gardens

For many travellers doing their "Grand Tour," the Mediterranean was not merely a history book or an inventory of monuments, but one of those "beautiful lands" which 16th-century Italians had depicted as a garden, and they returned with models of it in their heads and plants. The vogue of the Hispanic-cum-Moorish Italian garden spread as quickly as the fashion for the chinoiserie that filled the Goncourt brothers' drawing room. On the French Riviera, at the end of the 19th century, there was not a single major garden whose plan did not include one or more thematic gardens. In the 1910s and 1920s, however, interest in these objects of curiosity dwindled, just as travelling became something much more commonplace. Belle Epoque, French-style flower-beds had gone out of fashion. It was the turn of the Mediterranean and its colonies on the other shore.

This was the theme put forward by Delmas and Lavergne for the garden of the Alpes Maritimes pavilion at the World Fair of Decorative Arts held in 1925. Their plan won over those who were opposed to the "Cubist garden" that was the predominant feature of the fair. At last a real garden, and not those vile cement constructions with their painted trees and their chlorotic candelabras! J.C.N. Forestier, creator of the Bagatelle gardens, who had chaired the selection jury, had also travelled around the Mediterranean and adapted the well-ordered French garden to the teeming vocabulary, rich in detail, of the hectic gardens of Andalusia, Italy, Spain and Morocco. In Béziers, in southern France, in 1918, he had made a garden for one Joseph Guy, which combined French compartmentalization and its regular layouts with interplays of complex levels, a host of steps and stairs, ornamental pools and ponds, channels and spouts. Enclosed areas protected by grouped trees alternated with cleared spaces that conjured up both the gardens of the Generalife and the Moroccan *ryad*, with their harmonies of sustained color and their lively contrasts of light and shadow.

Later on, Forestier would apply these principles in Seville in Maria-Luisa Park, a mixture of the Generalife, the Alhambra and the Alcazar, in an unfurling of garden ceramics, pergolas, trellises, arbors and water channels plunged amid luxuriant vegetation. In a work titled *Gardens, Notebook of Plans and Designs* (1920), he put the case for colored compositions that would combine the freedom of the English garden with the geometric density of the *paradeisos*: "Close to a very white wall, there is a juxtaposition between the dark foliage of slender cypresses and the soft blooms of peach, almond and apricot and the purple flowers of

182

Roman fresco, Pompeii.
"Augustus," wrote Pierre Grimal, "had decorated the walls of his garden with delightful paintings depicting country houses, porticos, small clipped trees, woods, thickets, hills and all manner of landscapes."

bougainvillea, and the red of *Tecoma capensis*, with roses winding about their dark spindle shapes. Here, anemones and tulips are framed by thick myrtles; oleander bows over a support of white marble, sprouting their fresh flowers against a whitewashed wall above which bursts the pale blue of a clump of *Plumbago capensis*, or the deep and fierce blue of *ipomoea*." The garden of the Bastide du Roy on the French Riviera, which he designed in 1927 for the Count and Countess of Polignac, was organized in this way, like a colorful architecture with its yellow and white enclosure and its beds of deep-hued tulips. The "Mediterranean garden" was born.

"What it involves," wrote Ferdinand Bac, creator of Les Colombières at Menton, "is making a choice of shapes coming from the Mediterranean, stripping them of anything that boasts the oh-so-precise character of times, religions and reigns, and deriving therefrom a sufficiently clear synthesis to rediscover the ancestral sign that brings them all together in one single family, lapped by the same sea, the same climate and the same original culture." So the Mediterranean garden wouldn't try to recreate those ancient theme gardens which had amazed Maurice Barrès on a journey to Isola Bella, and described in *Of Blood, Voluptuousness and Death* (1893): "Those old groves, no longer with Armide and Alcine in them," he wrote, "still offer a profusion of plants from every manner of climate, and the formidable impression from terrace to terrace, because there is a different crop each time, but the harmony isn't destroyed by the mixture of disparate species, which is the drawback in botanical gardens. Abundant clumps of lemon and orange trees, camellias, camphor laurels, magnolias and cedars of Lebanon successively offer us the atmosphere of all the provinces of the southerly world"; rather, the Mediterranean garden strove to create a garden evoking only itself in a new entity.

One of the preferred motifs of the "Mediterranean garden" was interlacing ribbons, like, for example,

[Page 184] *The Villas of Bordighera*, (detail), 1884, Claude Monet.
Monet in Bordighera: a fairyland of half-wild gardens, a colorful shimmering so intense that the painter was worried that in Paris people would think he was mad.

[Page 185] The garden of Majorelle, in Marrakech.
Lost in an outlying neighborhood of Marrakech, the garden of paradise of the Nancy decorator —a painter in his day—and its famous morning glory blue walls.

pittosporum climbing through the olive tree, *floribonda* roses assaulting an arbor of wisteria, where jasmine has been allowed to sprawl. The waterway of the Generalife, the geometry of the Alhambra, the *azuleros* of Lisbon, the ponds of a Moroccan *ryad*, the pergolas of the Roman *villa rustica*, stairways flanked by the most sumptuous of columns and statues, and the terraces of the Medicis, are not there like collector's items, but as parts of one and the same world. Ferdinand Bac explains how this new garden imposed itself upon him: "I had gathered a large number of annotations on the art of building in Latin countries. I had engraved the most modest, and those with the minimum of artifice, on my memory, as those being most in tune with reason. It is from this slightly unusual ensemble that there emerged the renewal of an architectural formula in which you will find everything but architecture...It is an architecture of feeling...An art made up of all our nostalgic memories and of all the places where we might have liked to erect our tent and sojourn in the sweetness of the Beautiful and the power of the Simple...The elegance of the Mediterranean is straightforward; you can hold it in the palm of your hand."

Ferdinand Bac adds: the Mediterranean garden is not an eclectic garden, nor is it a regionalist garden; it is seeking a broader expression, akin to the "Mediterranean syncretism" for which the *Cahiers du Sud*, created in 1925, campaigned. "It was in no way a matter of slavishly copying Italian villas, he wrote, but of drawing inspiration from their experience, from the Spanish mystery, from the admirable Orient, father of those real gardens whose forms are mixed ad infinitum with our classical art and that, for a long time, have been established on our shore." The overall impression should be that of an age-old land where people have preserved woods of cypress, oak, olive and fig in the place where they had always been in accordance with the "disorderly order" that nature had ordained for them, and where people added to them everything that had enriched the Mediterranean landscape down the centuries. Marked by the sun, the garden was

187

[From left to right]
Garden in Vence.
Garden of the Mamounia, in Marrakech.
The triangular garden of Gabriel Guevrekian, 1928.
Pictorial or geometric: the Mediterranean garden.

bound to boast several sundials, but it also had to know how to protect itself with the help of wisteria-clad arbours. Its walls spilled over with roses from Bengal, bougainvillea and fruit trees. It would also open up prospects surveying the sea, create glimpses between cypresses, consider the morphology of an often steep-sided site, make the most of its espaliers, the better to reveal the savory irregularities. But this profusion must not obscure the rustic nature of the whole. It was banned from using excessively luxurious materials and useless ornaments. The Italian brickwork of pergolas and paths paved with stones and pebbles from fields…this was the essence of the Mediterranean.

Writers also contributed to the success of the Mediterranean garden, one such being Gide, who adored the "tall nettle-trees" in Clémence and Tancrède Gide's garden at Uzès, "crushing rose petals" in the company of Valéry in the avenues of the School of Medicine at Montpellier, wandering through "the dark gardens of the Cascini" in Florence, or biting the flesh of under-ripe lemons in the Latoniae at Syracuse, the true garden of *The Thousand and One Nights*. At La Treille Muscate, which she purchased in 1925 in the countryside near St. Tropez, Colette would describe the "peaceful miracles" of her summer garden, which she wanted to be like the little horticultural smallholdings in the hills of Grasse. At the same time, Bonnard went to live in Cannet, in a house surrounded by a garden whose riot of blooms he would then paint. The sweeping views he produced from the heights where Le Bosquet is located would evoke a rural golden age that likened the Riviera to the "beautiful land" of the ancients. After Gide and Paul Alibert, Francis Ponge would extol the garden of La Fontaine in Nimes in an anthological page, admiring "above all else the pink and gold aspect of the walls, steps and balustrades, paving stones and statues—that impulsive aspect, great and lively wall-hangings of pines rising in twists and turns at the garden's end to that final rose, like a magnolia flower, the Magne tower; those branches on the ground floor, arranged by a student of Le Nôtre, that aspect of clumps and bushes of roses arranged and composed with the structures and the stone; the magnificent, regal, sumptuous, scented character of this setting, incidentally adjoining the *garrigue*, in other words, dryness, aridity, austerity, and almost barrenness, but so ablaze, like Rome in the midst of its sterile countryside."

189

Details of the fresco in the Garden Room of the Villa Livia, near the Prima Porta in Pompeii.
The favorable place is enclosed, contrasting the seething bustle of wild nature with the emptiness of the cultivated space and its many walls.

Florette, Le Treyas, 1942,
Jaques-Henri Lartigue.
The paradise of coves and fortunate
islands before the invasion of the beach.

centuries to the skin of the Greeks, and is actually forcing them to leave these islands to seek work abroad. Anaphi, Pholegandro, Leros and Carros were also, in the 1970s, the obligatory residence of those who opposed the colonels and their regime. Therein," Lacarrière underscores, "lies a history that we tend to forget, or are even totally ignorant about, that dark side of those white islands, those bare rocks, those deserted beaches, that shimmering sea, all of which, here, are in no way places for romantic escapes, but sometimes places of escape, period." Armed with the Guidebook to the Mediterranean's isles of charm, the island-hopper who spends a day or a few hours on each one scarcely has the time to think of all this.

They are perhaps not quite as numerous as Bernard Lehembre might imagine, in the Blue Guide to the Greek islands, those people who "walk in the footsteps of their great instructors, be it Henry Miller on Poros, Lawrence Durrell on Corfu, Marguerite Yourcenar on Euboea or Rupert Brooke on Skyros." Since Michel Déon and his Le *Rendez-vous de Patmos*, everything happens as if the island were deserted by writers too. In his film *Caro Diario*, Nanni Moretti shoots the end of the island-as-haven. Venezzano, the

imaginary island of Julien Gracq's *The Opposing Shore*, was already nothing more than an "ambiguous and lugubrious" rock, surrounded by rocks of a "grey whiteness like bones," where Aldo and Vanessa meet one another "like two children stealing into a forbidden cellar." In the wake of Ulysses' companions on the island of the Lotus-eaters, they risk plunging into "a well of oblivion and slumber." From another angle, the Mediterranean island is still, as Robert Brasillach writes in *How Time Passes*, "the purest symbol man has managed to make of his happiness"; the very place of a reconciliation with the world, as invariably described in the tales of Erri De Luca at San Monato.

[Above] Liliane (Yveline Cery) and Juliette (Stefania Sabatini) on the boat sailing to Girolata, in *Adieu Philippine* by Jacques Rozier, 1963.
Refuge for a weekend or a lifetime: the Mediterranean myth is being sorely tried by disillusionment.

[Facing] Bay of Sagone, Corsica.

[Pages 202–203] *Blue II*, 1961, Joan Miró.
Mediterranean of islands and "sea voyages": a script to be deciphered.

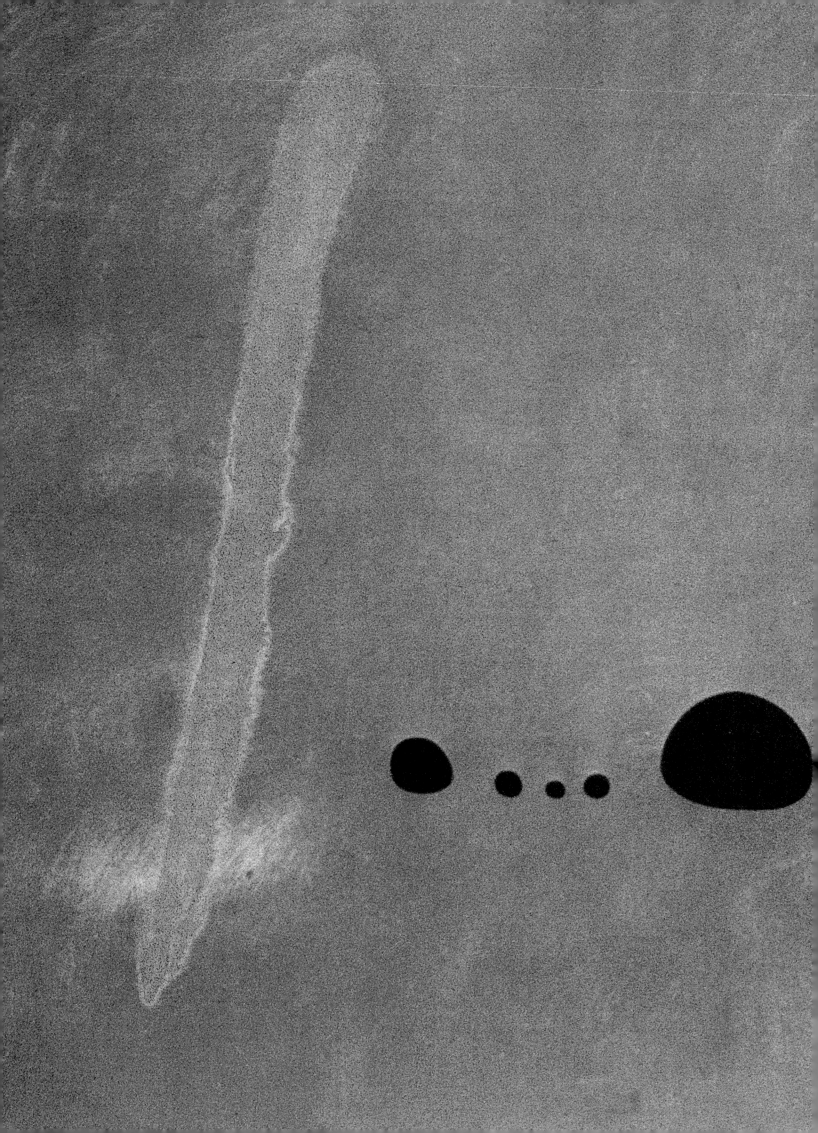

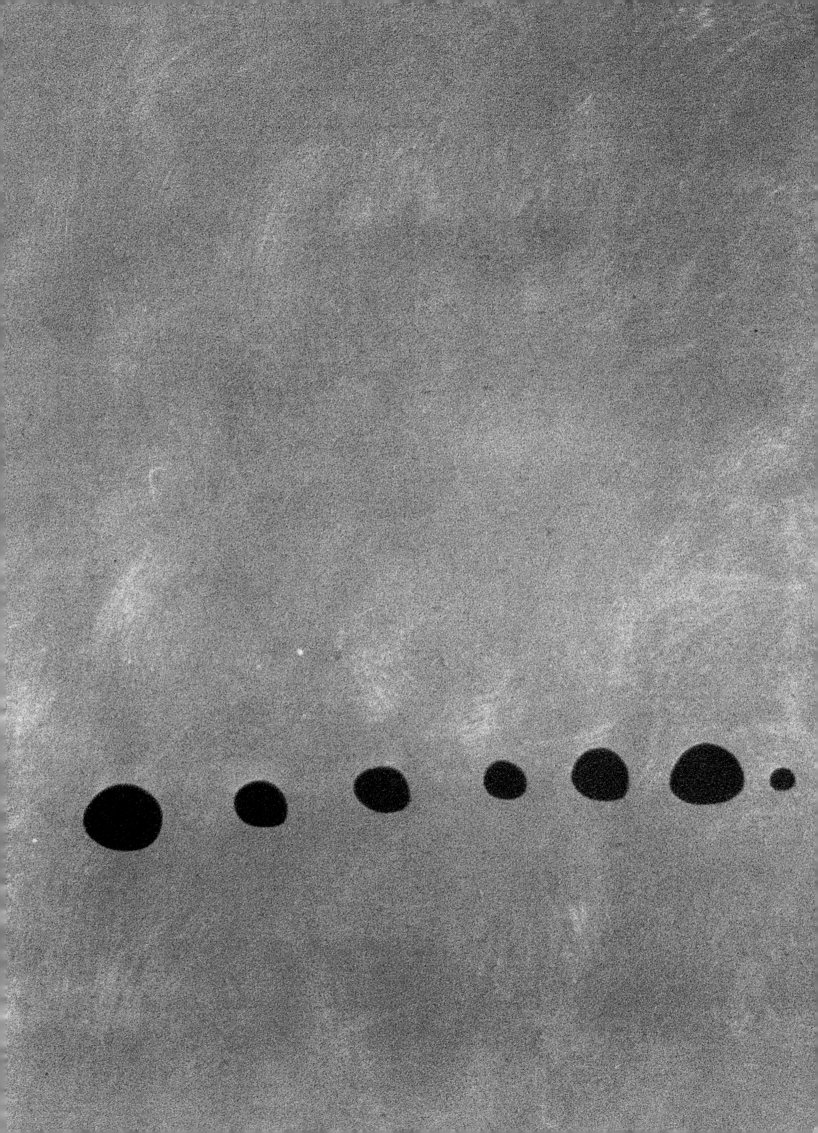

The Pillars of Hercules

The Arabs call it "the Narrow Gate," *Bab el-Zaka*. The ten miles or so that separate the square of the Grand Socco in Tangiers from the geraniums and pubs of Gibraltar bear this out, not only for the Arabs, but also for those attempting to make the watery crossing by night. The English call it, more prosaically, "the Gut." It has to be said that the Strait of Gibraltar doesn't always stir the imagination. No monument or major event draws our attention to it. The rock conquered by the intrepid Tariq—who invaded the Iberian peninsula in 711, starting from these southern shores (Gibraltar actually means "the Mountain of Tariq," *Geb el-Tariq*)—with its 1,395 foot crag and its colony of Barbary apes, is not a particularly thrilling sight. The Phoenicians, who were the first to negotiate the strait on behalf of the Egyptians, heading for the shores of Africa and Cornwall, called it one of the "pillars of Melkarth," the god of Hell, on the edge of the known world. The other "pillar" lay in the direction of Abyla, but there was nothing to be done about the fact that the "gate" was annoyingly asymmetrical. The entrance to the Mediterranean had nothing triumphal about it. You had to be a denizen of Tangiers and Paul Bowles to have the bright idea of composing a cantata to the strait titled *Through the Strait*. At the end of the epic journey made by Hercules, the "glorious conqueror" would lend his name to the Phoenicians' pillars, even though those large, wind-worn boulders hardly look like marble pillars.

The Arabs also invented a mythical reason for the separation of the two continents. A late 18th-century traveller and diplomat, Abu Kacem al-Zayyân described in his diary, *The Turjumânâ*, the time when Spain and Morocco formed a single landmass: "The Andalusians, victims of Berber attacks, complained to Alexander, who ordered his engineers and technicians to dig the strait...This is how the Mediterranean was filled in...And peace was restored to the Andalusians."

But which gate was it? "The Atlantic on one side, the Mediterranean on the other," wrote Robert Briatte in his book about Paul Bowles. "People have never been able to make up their minds, so they called it 'the strait.' A sound not easy to navigate, but busy, especially where it is deep." Two contradictory reactions are pointed out, often to stress both its narrowness and the proximity between Andalusia and Africa—like Michel del Castillo in his *Andalusia*: "You finally cross the strait getting an idea about how slight the frontier separating the two continents is. It is not surprising to learn that the Iberians, the earliest inhabitants of Andalusia, were Berbers from Africa, if we are to believe the anthropologists. From the ferry gangway, the eye strays from the peaks of the Rif to those of the Sierra Nevada." And to emphasize the moat that separates the two worlds,

204

Tangiers. View over the Strait of Gibraltar, 1985.
From the Andalusian plains to Morocco: "Same flora, same light, same arrangement of towns and villages, same fauna," wrote Michel del Castillo, but two worlds separated by the Mediterranean.

This verdict is contradicted by those who defend a Mediterranean art of living, and are never short of supporting arguments; nutritionists have recently made the inhabitants of Crete models of longevity thanks to olive oil, grilled eggplants, tomatoes and barbecued fish. Wine has acquired unsuspected virtues and ancestral forms of bread still have no serious rivals. The siesta is an invention of the gods. As a sign of the times, the appearance of the heading "arts of living" in guidebooks is quite recent. Books describe "the art of living" in Venice, Naples, Rome, Istanbul and Marrakech, as if life in these cities had remained unchanged since the golden age of the urban aristocracy. The South is no longer merely synonymous with Robinson Crusoe-like escapades, swimming and bathing; people live in the South in accordance with very ancient rules governing the social graces, in painstakingly restored homes. Provençal country homes, Venetian palaces, *yalis* on the Bosphorus, Moroccan *ryads*, Andalusian haciendas: living by the Mediterranean is to link up once more with untrammelled traditions, surround yourself with objects unearthed in antique shops at Isle-sur-la-Sorgue and Seville, and fantasize about a somewhat archaistic and sophisticated Mediterranean. It is also to sing the praises of a "sunny," convivial, colorful style of cooking, with generous flavors, which glorifies the tastes of

220

[Above, left to right]
Still from Marcel Pagnol's *Marius*, 1931.
Naxos, Greece.
Still from the film *Marius and Jeannette*, Robert Guédiguian, 1997.
The convivial friendliness of the South, a ready-made image and a truth shared "Marseilles-style."

produce from the local market and lives in symbiosis with the seasonal rhythms: as in Venice, where people eat dry fruit *pinza* in January, fritters at carnival time, roast kid goat at Easter, risotto in April, crunchy almond biscuits at Ascension, and chicken casserole at Christmas. Or Istanbul, where people savor broad beans called *lüfer* in the autumn; Siliuri yogurt in late winter; *salep*, that hot milk drink perfumed with orchid roots, with the approach of winter; and for the festival celebrating the end of Ramadan, that orgy of sweets that are called *cheker hayramï*. These traditions are more tenacious than they might seem: a little local restaurant in Old Nice would never let All Saints' day go by without preparing its "soup of the dead." There is a seasonal cuisine in the Mediterranean, but also a distinctly geographical cuisine, too, as the famous French chef Alain Ducasse is at pains to let us know, indefatigable champion that he is of Taggia olives, rice from the Po valley, white truffles from Alba, hazelnuts from Piedmont, small black pichouline olives from the hills behind Nice, ricotta from Roman ewes, and Sardinian artichokes with their prickly leaves. Casanova, for his part, consumed his fill of "bread from Padua, wine from Vicenza, tripe from Treviso and women from Venice." The Mediterranean art of living is something at once exotic and yet very close to hand.

221

[Page 222] The wedding of Simone Signoret and Yves Montand at the Colombe d'Or, in 1951.

[Page 223] *Large Red Interior*, 1948, Henri Matisse.
"You know, my passion, that purple and already ripe, each pomegranate bursts." (Stéphane Mallarmé)

Arts

"What is the Mediterranean imagination? What is Mediterranean literature? What is it that typifies creative work in the Mediterranean?" wonders Baltasar Porcel in *Mediterranean, Turmoil of the Swell*, while at the same time lamenting the fact that, as yet, there has been no satisfactory answer to these oh-so-simple questions. "There is a School of Vienna," he rails, "and nobody recognizes a single decisive Mediterranean substance!" According to this author, such a substance has surely existed and been at work in the Mediterranean since the late 19th century, among painters born on its shores like Picasso, Dalí, Miró and De Chirico, and those hailing from the north and subsequently "Mediterraneanized" once in contact with it, like Turner, Van Gogh, Klee, Chagall, Matisse, Bonnard and many more.

But isn't the opposite every bit as accurate? Bonnard transposes to Le Cannet the vision of a lush and verdant Normandy. Returning home to Veronet, the light of the Midi suffuses the Norman pictures. It is said of Signac that he "Marseillified the suburbs" of Paris. In Vence, Chagall was always the painter from Vitebsk. The golden light with which Turner shrouded Venice conjures up Norham Castle more than the morning clarity of the paintings of Carpaccio and Canaletto. In Tangiers, Matisse discovered "a true Normandy in the Orient." Provence would forever remind Van Gogh of Holland and the Japan of those Ukiyo E. prints.

In order to single out this "Mediterranean substance," which is so specific—and, as we can see, so mixed— Porcel sadly also makes the traditional arguments about the "spellbinding color" and "joyous and orgiastic chromatism, humanized and full of fantasy," which hallmarked Miró's work. The Mediterranean, "realm of color," is an invention, just like the whiteness of the marble of "Ideal Beauty." The 19th-century painters of Marseilles, like Loubon and Guigou, did not depict the environs of the city in brighter hues than those used by Lebourg for the environs of Rouen. The German Expressionist painters didn't need to stay in Collioure to portray the shores of the North Sea, like Schmidt-Rottluff at Dangast, in fiery purples and blacks. Of course, wrote Porcel, "on Miró's canvas black also reigns, that fearsome color of tragedy beneath the sun"; needless to say, Picasso's art was an art of cruelty, but the cruelty was no more Spanish than happiness, hedonism and bright colors are Mediterranean (even if we find them here in profusion...). Was the little Surrealist theatre that Dalí organized on the beaches of Port Lligat more Mediterranean than the world of Max Ernst or André Masson?

So what is this specific quality of Mediterranean creativity if the sea, the sun, the dazzling light and the beauty of things do not define just it alone? Does the answer lie in this dark Mediterranean, in this twofold tragedy

Photo-collage, to Pablo Picasso, with a dedication by Jacques Prévert and André Villers.
Portrait of the artist in the clown-yellow sun; Picasso's masks: more than a game among friends,
a creative method derived from the sources of the pre-classical Mediterranean.

A PABLO PICASSO
son ami
Jacques Prévert
et
André Villers

invoked by so many authors to defend a sea that postcards haven't once and for all repainted in holiday hues? Or alternatively, as Camus suggested, in that wavering between these two poles: the glorification of life and the sense of tragedy? The ancient threnody of a female Sicilian singer and the strident utterance of the male raï singer? Not so long ago, the latest developments of modern life in the Mediterranean inspired Thierry Fabre to write a beautiful piece, wonderfully summed up by its title, *Black and Blue*. But black is not the only sign of the tragic, the Mafia, fundamentalism and wild brands of nationalism, nor blue the sole color of dreams, hopes and an "open identity." Homer never described the sea as having a blue color; the *kynaeos* was a glassy paste with which people rendered the walls of palaces; the sea, for its part, was "like violet" or "wine-red." And in the Arab-Muslim world, isn't white the color of mourning, and black, the most intense of colors for Velazquez, Manet and even Matisse?

Any attempt to verify the existence of a "Mediterranean substance" and its opposite components turns out to be as illusory as any belief in a Mediterranean "being." More helpfully, Roland Barthes puts forward the hypothesis, with regard to Cy Twombly, of a "Mediterranean effect," suggesting that its action mobilizes "a huge complex of memories and sensations," as well as "an historical, mythological, poetic culture."

We are brought to this effect by Miró's *The Farm*. The picture was started in the summer of 1921 in the village of Montroig, a dozen miles or so south of Tarragona, in Catalonia. Back in Barcelona, Miró worked further on it; he would put the finishing touches to it in Paris, on the Rue Blomet, where he set up home that same autumn. This exile's itinerary would lend the work a recapitulative function, as if the painter had carried away with him the total image of his country. *The Farm* is a treasure, the reliquary of a "lost countryside." "It is almost," wrote Robert Hughes in his *Barcelona*, "a pictorial form of those meticulous inventories that go with the marriage contracts of countryfolk. Each tool, pitcher, cask, press, cart, watering-can, donkey, dog, chicken, goat, pigeon and ass's rump... is brought into the light, dissected, noted and set down." Like the buildings described by Henri Bosco, Miró's *The Farm* is a "moral edifice," it puts on the same level the rose of the watering can and the moon hanging in the sky, the inside of the chicken coop and the cracks on the façade, the bark of the eucalyptus and the tree itself. This plethora of details likens it to the landscapes of Ambrogio Lorenzotti, and the crags of Andrea Mantegna and Fra Filippo Lippi. Everything here, as in certain parts of the Mediterranean, is of equal majesty. Perhaps this is the "Mediterranean effect" of the work, this extravagance of sharp and solid objects, this sort of shearing of contours, which makes the whole land hum beneath an evenly blue sky.

But it is also possible to qualify as Mediterranean, precisely contrasting with aesthetics and the "détailliste" viewpoint, the enveloping color of certain works. In Kairouan, Klee had just such an experience: "Color takes possession of me," he wrote. "There is no point whatsoever in trying to grasp it. It possesses me, I know it. This is the meaning of the happy moment: color and me are one. I am a painter." Matisse's Tangiers paintings were also of this ilk. *Landscape Seen from the Window*—which the painter would also call *Blue Landscape*—and *The Gate of the Casbah* introduce us to a Mediterranean of diaphanous, delicious, invading color, bounced back by the white walls of the Arab city, and the tall trees of the garden. The chapel in Vence bore the mark of this

226

Man Walking, 1960, Alberto Giacometti.
Every summer, on the terrace of the Maeght Foundation, near St. Paul-de-Vence, amid the heady rasping of cicadas, Giacometti's Man Walking, *like some ingenious hidalgo, confronting the windmills of the Coast.*

revelation, which had been shored up by his stay in Tahiti: color would be the real subject, a climatic, immaterial color, as impalpable and elusive as the diffused blue and milky green of the paintings produced during his Moroccan sojourn. One of them would be red. Matisse told Gothard Jedlicka: "Finding myself on one occasion in the chapel, I noticed on the floor a red that was so material that I had the feeling that the color was not the effect of the light coming in from the window, but that it was connected with a material. A particular circumstance reinforced this impression. On the ground, before me, there was some sand, arranged in a little heap on which this red had been set. It had the effect of a magnificent red powder, such as I had never before encountered in all my life. I stooped towards it. I put my hand in the sand, I extracted a handful and brought it up to my eyes, and I made it run between my fingers: a grey substance. But I haven't forgotten that red, and one day I'd like to manage to bring it to my canvas."

In Florence, Claudel described a similar sensation: "The first thing that immediately filled me, through my eyes," he wrote, "like a liquid, was the blue. There is nothing as blue as Florence. In other regions and lands, blue is, well, you know, the sky, and you never get the idea that you can walk in it. But here, blue covers and fills everything." In Venice, who has not experienced that euphoria of an ambient color on the borderline between pink and green? Or in Jerusalem, when the city walls turn golden ochre? Many Mediterranean colors can be compared with these: it's impossible to hold them fast, they are in the air of a city, a magic suspense, a revelation of happiness.

The work of Antonio Gaudí is both a brightly colored atmosphere and a riot of details; you venture into it as into a cave or grotto, or the entrails of some monster, and you find yourself forever appraising in detail the thousand and one arabesques of its miniature settings. This is a way of simultaneously giving the speech of both a decorator and an architect, of putting yourself in the middle of things, in accordance with the definition of a Mediterranean art provided by Gaudí himself: "Virtue is located at the central point; Mediterranean means in the middle of the earth. It is on its shores, where an average light shafts down at 45°, defining and best showing the form of bodies, that the great artistic cultures have thrived, in this harmony of light: not too much, not too little...; it is in the Mediterranean that the concrete vision of things holds sway, that vision on which real art must be based." Like the siting of the Greek sanctuary, the place where the sacred edifice rises up must be situated in the center of a symbolic topography. "In the Sagrada Familia," Gaudí observed, "everything is providence; the temple is situated at the center of the city and plateau of Barcelona; the same distance separates it from the sea and the mountains, from Sants and from San Andres, and the Beros and Llobregat rivers." Gaudí's aesthetic also postulates a center, halfway between the Gothic West and the Far East, between Spanish mysticism and the mysticism of Wagner, between Mediterranean joyfulness and the penitence of the reconquest. As a conservative Catholic and a brilliant experimenter, a Catalan and a universal everyman, Gaudí dreamed of a great synthetic form that would bring together within itself all the ingredients of creation. The model of this huge collage might be that of the *trencadis*, those bits of ceramics that are broken and then reassembled, with which he covered every conceivable kind of surface.

229

Joan Miró in his studio in Majorca.
"Down with the Mediterranean!—I shouted that" (during the famous Surrealists' banquet in honour of Saint Pol Roux at the Closerie des Lilas), Miró told Georges Raillard, "because we were numbed by all the people forever stuffing our skulls with the Mediterranean, the innocence, the harmony, the moderation and all those stories."

Viallat's work likewise puts the painter at the center of a potentially "immense" world, endlessly overwhelmed by an intense multicoloredness and the harmonic repetition of the same form, "the simplest, the most elementary, and the most immediate there could be." Here, the Mediterranean has the same function of symbolic environment, from which the painter can branch out in all directions. This manner of putting yourself in the middle of the work, as at the center of a native land, within a space which calls for a veritable hand-to-hand tussle, was often associated with Villat's fondness for bullfighting. Same sun-drenched colors, same unfurling of fabrics with colorful undersides, same accelerations, same calculated decelerations and studied forms of negligence: there is no shortage of comparisons, all expressing the dream of a proximity between the painter's work and the passions of the South.

Like Viallat's work, the sculpture of Pagès lives in symbiosis with a Mediterranean environment from which it borrows not only its materials but also its skills and its favorite motifs. Pagès' work is at once arid and flamboyant, with an intense polychromatic aspect and teeming design, tousled and overgrown and yet governed by a rigid geometry, in perpetual motion and also showing a stony motionlessness. It nevertheless defies any kind of belonging to a regionalist vein, as it does any claim to identity. It is certainly Mediterranean, but in the same way as a certain use of light, straightforward colors, open air and inventions cobbled together in an economy of penury.

The Mediterranean summoned up by the postmodern generation is quite different. Here, models play a predominant part. Ricardo Bofill reinstates the images of an ancient architecture in huge theatrical re-creations, while the Italian artists of the *Transavanguardia* group veer towards De Chirico, Carra and Sironi, as well as Giotto and Piero della Francesca, to present a Mediterranean where, in many instances, pathos ill disguises the little factory of kitsch images. In the mid-1980s, Jean-Charles Blais conjured up a Mediterranean that had been relieved of that surplus of pictorial references, in drawings produced on the Riviera and in Morocco. In them, the gigantic figures that brought the artist to public attention at the end of the 1980s are separated from their suddenly cumbersome appearance, and become lost in the landscape of the sheet of paper invaded by the dazzling blue of Midi skies.

Countless photographers also attempt to grasp and capture this captionless Mediterranean, over and above the lure of the panoramic vista, in a kind of espoused void, like Gabriele Basilico, photographer of cities and people-free seasides, huddled around their own secrets. The Mediterranean myth of a world split between luxuriant garden of Eden and theatrical inferno gives way to a commonplace Mediterranean, photographed the wrong way round, almost colorless, running counter to the saturated imagery of tourism. It's a Mediterranean on the edge of hallowed sites, lit by a naked daylight, which surges up from this amazing reverse shot. The back is often turned to the sea either to penetrate the spaces of private intimacy, or to venture into the labyrinth of unbridled urban growth. Artists like Bustamante show the construction site of new residential areas with the same obsessive objectivity as if what was involved was industrial documents. Richard Baquié presents a Marseilles-oriented South which owes nothing to the beauty of Provence.

The Mediterranean, that still inspired fashion designers of the 1980s such as Christian Lacroix, is becoming more distant. Azzedine Alaïa pursues his solo journey inspired by the Tunisia of his childhood, in an immense

[Page 232] Dalí and Gala swimming at Port Lligat, with Vermeer's *The Lacemaker*, 1959. *The Lacemaker (without horns) between Dalí and Gala, in August 1967, at Cabo Crus, near Cadaques, during the shooting of* The Miraculous Tale of The Lacemaker and the Rhinoceros: *an illustration of the painter's paranoid criticism according to which* The Lacemaker *was a rhinoceros horn with curves as perfect as a (bent) sunflower, a cauliflower or a sea urchin.*

diwan of East and West. Dolce & Gabbana's images of Sicily have been put away with the accessories. Part of a Mediterranean recipe is changing. Almodovar isn't making a scandal any more. Mediterranean design, a synonym for sensuality, Baroque-inspired style and warm colors, is looking for a new identity. If it is drawing from the same stock as it has over the past two decades, this is to mix in the eclectic motifs of a more open-minded culture. Not so very long ago, to make something Mediterranean required turning not to Mediterranean people themselves, but to the great models which writers and artists from the North had constructed: "The erotic-cum-literary setting," wrote Ohran Pamuk, "needed Gustav von Aschenbach in Thomas Mann's *Death in Venice*, Edward Morgan Forster's *Where Angels Fear to Tread*, Tennessee Williams' *The Roman Spring of Mrs. Stone*, and Paul Bowles' *The Sheltering Sky*," just like painters needed Matisse, Klee and Léger to express the South.

These days, anyone gauging creative activity in the Mediterranean must blaze their trail among the cultures of the countries hemming the Inland Sea. If the Mediterranean of those 20th-century masters who sought refuge amid its gardens still lives in the minds of many, all that is needed is a stroll around the museums of the Riviera, or a visit, one winter's day, to the Maeght Foundation, near St. Paul, to be persuaded that another Mediterranean has been taking shape since the 1960s. No longer that sumptuous Mediterranean resembling some Oriental dream of Matisse in his Regina apartments in Nice, or Picasso's Mediterranean, still haunted by Antiquity, at Notre-Dame-de-Vie, nor the mythological Mediterranean of Cocteau, nor even the dreamy, solar Mediterranean of Miró, but one of Mediterranean writers and artists. "Our own vision of the Mediterranean is so natural to us," wrote Thierry Fabre and Robert Ilbert, "that we readily forget that it is above all a mental construct, that is part and parcel of an historical and cultural genealogy peculiar to each country."

The "scrub" and "sticks" towards which artists of the last century gravitated no longer exists. Unless he lets himself be steered about by guidebooks describing the sites and monuments, the traveller who goes to Morocco can no longer overlook the fact that he is in the land of Driss Chraibi, Mohamed Choukri, Fatima Mernissi, Abdellatif Laâbi and many more. He no longer photographs a territory given over to just the way the travel photograph sees things, but the world that has been so wonderfully seen by Touhami Ennadre and Daoud Aoulad in their book *Moroccans*, or Souad Guennoun, surveyor of the streets of Casablanca. He no longer conceives of a country devoid of intellectuals, but of the land of Mohamed Tozy, Abdou Filaly and Hinde Taärji, among many others. The same goes for the countries that are currently in evidence on the Mediterranean cultural stage. The Mediterranean confined within its history and its heritage, a prisoner of its centuries-old rivalries and its North-South axis, can still nurture the thought processes of the European who is worried about his and its future. The culture of the Mediterranean countries that is under construction today describes it in a different light. More complex, informed by inventiveness rather than fear, less concerned with making way for a shared hypothetical identity than with creating works that merely lay claim to their sole singularity: the artistic Mediterranean is no longer a school day recollection and memory, or a unifying utopia, but a living reality, and one that is stronger than ever.

231

[Page 233] Matisse in his studio.
Matisse at the window of one of his Mediterranean apartment-cum-studios, the conventional image of the great classical painter at work.

Epilogue

At the end of our ramble, what image of the Mediterranean remains? What symbol? What predominant figure? That of Cross's picture called *The Isles of Gold*, which tells us of a slack sea in the glowing light of a summer's morn? Or alternatively that of Picasso's "Baigneuses insectivores," on a beach resembling a training camp? Is it the "lovable blue" Mediterranean of those Romantic—and romantic—travellers of yore, or the dark Mediterranean of Buñuel? Gaudí's multicolored, Baroque version, or the classical all-white version of Winckelmann? That of Giono's half-invented countryfolk in the Provence of *Jean le Bleu* or those faithfully described by Carlo Levi in the rugged mountains of Lucania? The "Mediterranean of the poor" conjured up by Georges Duby with its sunny ferocity, or that of odalisques and "art of living" magazines? The Mediterranean of the Riviera in the 1960s conjured up by Martial Raysse, in the form of a beach stall selling knickknacks, or the selfsame Mediterranean, a few years later, turned into an ancient landscape?

We could have elected to cross-question Cross's Mediterranean as opposed to Picasso's, that of the *Joie de vivre* as opposed to that of *Guernica*. But as Flaubert learnt during his Oriental journeys, the Mediterranean is always and invariably both the one and the other, sometimes in the very same shot. Did I dream up that image of Beirut at war with those beaches where people still played football in their swimming costumes? Or those seaside photographs near Viareggio in Tuscany, filled with bathers, a stone's throw from huge factory chimneys? The "isles of mauve silk, sparkling and transparent, weightless and almost shapeless, fading to the wavy line of their faintly delineated ridges," described by Giono in *The Horseman on The Roof*, belong to the same image as the blotchy, bluish bodies of victims of epidemics.

There exists in the Mediterranean an art of catastrophe, a staging and presentation of tragedy which is part of the legacy. In his book *Run on the Wild Shore*, Mohammed Dib shows two of his characters "in the midst of people, also in beach wear, busy gathering arms, legs and torsos scattered on the sand... There is nothing sad about their task," the author adds, "and nothing macabre. The scattered limbs and busts, larger than life, have such perfect lines that they seem to have belonged to godheads. This must be what

234

removes any impression of horror from this sight." The foreground of a crucifixion by Antonello da Messina is also covered with scattered limbs. The light caressing them is one of the gentlest imaginable. A few years ago, an Algerian photo of a *Pietà* made the rounds of the press agencies; it wasn't merely tragic, it was beautiful; the photo hailed from the Algerian tragedy. But wasn't it too beautiful to have been taken live? No matter. The fact is that the *Pietà* is still there—part of the heritage as well.

Our representations of the Mediterranean are of this ilk; we still see it from another image with which we make our compromises, like our Italian travellers. What Fernand Braudel said about Venice applies to the Mediterranean as well: "We have imagined it far too much before getting to know it, in order to see it as it is. We like it through ourselves. Spell, illusion, trap, distorting mirrors, that's what it is; what we ask it to be."

Here we've reached the final image of "our sea," which is also one of the most euphoric I know. It has been with me throughout this book: it is the image of the cup of Exekias, on view in the Museum of Antiquities in Munich. The scene depicts Dionysos crowned with ivy, lying down in the middle of a fish-shaped ship, in the posture of a guest at a banquet. But Dionysos is alone in the middle of the sea on a boat with no helmsman. He lets himself be moved across a perfectly smooth expanse of water—Homer's "never harvested sea"—where seven dolphins frolic and romp. From the middle of the vessel rises a mast with a vine coiled about it, with seven huge bunches of grapes. The story goes that Dionysos had embarked incognito on a pirate ship and was captured and lashed to the mast. After freeing himself from his ropes, there was an extraordinary sequence of events: "First and foremost it was wine, that mild perfumed beverage which spilled over the swift black deck," then "a vine branch unfurled on either side, up to the top of the sail, from where hung many bunches of grapes." Around the mast, you could also see the ivy clinging "laden with flowers": it was then that the terrified sailors flung themselves into the sea where they were turned into dolphins. The adventure is a challenge to the "infertile plain" and its divisions; Dionysos, who was not averse to the odd facetious remark, transported his garden there along with the banquet couch, so that he could literally live, in his own home, in the Mediterranean.

Bibliography

General works

ADAM, Jean-Pierre, *La Méditerranée*, Paris, Castermann, 1985.
BRAUDEL, Fernand, *La Méditerranée et le monde méditerranéen à l'époque de Philippe II*, Paris, A. Colin, 1967-1990;
Le Modèle italien, Paris, Arthaud, 1989; *Autour de la Méditerranée*, Paris, Éd. de Fallois, 1996;
Les Mémoires de la Méditerranée: préhistoire et antiquité, Paris, Éd. de Fallois, 1997;
Venise, Paris, Arthaud, 1997, photos by Folco Quilici.
FABRE, Thierry, *La Méditerranée entre la raison et la foi*, Arles, Actes Sud, Babel, 1998;
La Méditerranée, frontières et passages, Arles, Actes Sud, Babel, 1999.
FLAHAUT, Dominique, *Il était une fois la Méditerranée : une mer en souffrance*, Paris, Flers, Équilibres d'aujourd'hui, 1991.
GRENIER, Jean, *Inspirations méditerranéennes*, Paris, Gallimard, 1961.
KAYSER, Bernard, *Méditerranée, une géographie de la fracture*, Aix-en-Provence, Édisud, 1996.
MATVEJEVITCH, Predrag, *Bréviaire méditerranéen*, translated by Evaine Le Calvé-Ivicevic, Paris, Payot-Rivages, 1995.
MORAND, Paul, *Méditerranée, mer des surprise*, Tours, Mame, 1938.
PIRENNE, Henri, *Mahomet et Charlemagne*, Paris, PUF, Quadrige, 1992.
SAID, Edward, *L'Orientalisme, L'Orient créé par l'Occident*, Paris, Le Seuil, 1980.
SIEGFRIED, André, *Vue générale de la Méditerranée*, Paris, Gallimard, 1943.

Collective works

La Méditerranée, l'espace et l'histoire, edited by Fernand Braudel, Paris, Flammarion, Champs, 1985.
La Méditerranée, les hommes et l'héritage, edited by Fernand Braudel and Georges Duby, Paris, Flammarion, Champs, 1986.
La Méditerranée, with contributions from Sigurd von Boletsky, Felix Karlinger, Hans Kühner, Franca Magnani, Lausanne-Paris, La Bibliothèque des arts, 1981.
France Europe du Sud, Géographie universelle, edited by Roger Brunet, with contributions from Robert Ferras, Denise Pomain, Thérèse Saint-Julien, Hachette/Belin/Reclus, 1990.
L'Invention scientifique de la Méditerranée, edited by Marie-Noëlle Bourguet, Bernard Lepetit, Daniel Nordman, Maroula Sinarellis, Éd. de l'EHESS, Paris, 1998.
Les Représentations de la Méditerranée, edited by Thierry Fabre and Robert Ilbert, Paris, Maisonneuve & Larose, 2000.
Méditerranées, an anthology introduced by Michel Le Bris and Jean Claude Izzo, Étonnants Voyageurs, Librio, 1998.
La Méditerranée créatrice, edited by Thierry Fabre, La Tour-d'Aigues, Éd. de l'Aube, 1992.
L'Héritage andalou, edited by Thierry Fabre, La Tour-d'Aigues, Éd. de l'Aube, 1994.

Periodicals
L'ARC, Les Cahiers du Sud, Alain Paire, Chronique des Cahiers du Sud, 1914-1966, Éd. IMEC, Paris, 1993;
Revue Passerelles; La Métis; Mediterraeans; Études méditerranéennes; XX siècle; Autre Sud; Quantara.

Travel works

BERCHET, J.-C., *Le Voyage en Orient*, an anthology of French travellers in the Orient in the 19th century, Paris, Robert Laffont, Bouquins, 1985.
CASTILLO, Michel del, *Andalousie*, Paris, Seuil, 1991.
FLAUBERT, *Œuvres*, Paris, Gallimard, Bibliothèque de La Pléiade, 1975-1977.
GOETHE, *Voyage en Italie*, translated by Mutterer, Genève-Paris, Slatkine, 1990.
GOYTISOLO, Juan, *À la recherche de Gaudí en Cappadoce*, Paris, Fayard, 1992.

GRACQ, Julien, *Autour des sept collines*, Paris, José Corti, 1988.

LACARRIÈRE, Jacques, *L'Été grec*, Paris, Plon, 1975; *En cheminant avec Hérodote*, Paris, Seghers, 1981;
Chemin faisant, followed by *La Mémoire des routes*, Paris, Fayard, 1997.

LOTI, Pierre, *Au Maroc*, Saint-Cyr-sur-Loire, Christian Pirot, 1990.

MAGRIS, Claudio, *Danube*, Paris, L'Arpenteur, 1988.

MONTAIGNE, *Journal de voyage en Italie par la Suisse et l'Allemagne en 1580-1581*, Paris, Les Belles Lettres, 1946.

NOOTEBOOM, Cees, *Désir d'Espagne, mes détours vers Santiago*, Arles, Actes Sud, 1993.

RONDEAU, Daniel, *Alexandrie*, Paris, Nil, 1997.

STENDHAL, *Voyages en Italie*, Paris, Gallimard, Bibliothèque La Pléiade, 1973.

SUARÈS, André, *Voyage du Condottière*, Granit, 1984, Provence, Édisud, 1993.

THEROUX, Paul, *Les Colonnes d'Hercule, voyage autour de la Méditerranée*, Paris, Grasset & Fasquelle, 1997.

WAUGH, Evelyn, *Bagages enregistrés, journal de voyage en Méditerranée*, Paris, Quai Voltaire, 1988.

Literary works

Les Mille et Une Nuits, translated by J.-C. Mardrus, Paris, Robert Laffont, Bouquins, 1995; translated by R.R. Khawam,
Paris, Phébus, 1986; *Les Dames de Bagdad*, translated by A. Miquel, Paris, Desjonquières, 1991.

AUDISIO, Gabriel, *La Vie de Harun el-Raschid*, Paris, Gallimard, 1930; *Jeunesse de la Méditerranée*, Paris, Gallimard, 1935;
Ulysse ou l'intelligence, Paris, Gallimard, 1945.

BARRÈS, Maurice, *L'Œuvre de Maurice Barrès*, Paris, Club de l'honnête homme, 1965-1968.

BOSCO, Henri, *Le Mas Théotime*, Paris, Gallimard, 1968; *Sites et Mirages*, Paris, Gallimard, 1951.

BOWLES, Paul, *Un thé au Sahara*, Paris, Gallimard, 1986; *Réveillon à Tanger*, Paris, Quai Voltaire, 1987.

BRASILLACH, Robert, *Comme le temps passe*, Paris, Plon, 1989.

BYRON, George, *Le Pèlerinage de Childe Harold*, Paris, M.P. Trémois, 1930.

CAMUS, Albert, *Noces*, suivi de *Eté*, Paris, Gallimard, Folio, 1959;
Œuvres, Paris, Gallimard, Bibliothèque de La Pléiade, 1962-1982.

CERVANTÈS, Miguel de, *L'Ingénieux Hidalgo Don Quichotte de la Manche*, translated by Aline Schulman, Paris, Seuil, 1997.

CONNOLLY, Cyril, *Marée basse*, Paris, Christian Bourgeois, 1988.

DELACROIX, Eugène, *Journal, 1822-1863*, Paris, Le Grand Livre du mois, 1998.

DÉON, Michel, *Pages grecques*, Paris, Gallimard, 1983; *"Je vous écris d'Italie…"*, Paris, Gallimard, 1984.

DIB, Mohammed, *Les Terrasses d'Orsol*, Paris, Sindbad, 1985; *Qui se souvient de la mer*, Paris, Seuil, 1990;
Au café, Arles, Actes Sud, 1996; *La Grande Maison*, Paris, Seuil, 1996.

DJAOUT, Tahar, *L'Invention du désert*, Paris, Seuil, 1987; *Les Vigiles*, Paris, Seuil, 1991.

DU CAMP, Maxime, *Le Nil*, Paris, Sand : Conti, 1987.

DURAS, Marguerite, *Le Marin de Gibraltar*, Paris, Gallimard, 1952; *Les Petits Chevaux de Tarquinia*, Paris, Gallimard, 1953.

DURRELL, Lawrence, *L'Île de Prospero*, Paris, Buchet/Chastel, 1962; *Le Quatuor d'Alexandrie*, Paris, Buchet/Chastel, 1970;
Citrons acides, Paris, Buchet/Chastel, 1971; *L'Ombre infinie de César, Regards sur la Provence*, Paris, Gallimard, Folio, 1994.

FAIK, Sait Abasiyanik, *Un point sur la carte*, Paris, Souffles, 1988.

FERRAOUN, Mouloud, *Les Chemins qui montent*, Paris, Seuil, 1987.

FLAUBERT, Gustave, *Carthage*, Paris, Stock, 1995; *Lettres d'Orient*, Bordeaux, L'Horizon chimérique, 1990;
Voyage en Égypte, Paris, Entente, 1986.

GIDE, André, *Œuvres*, Paris, Gallimard, Bibliothèque de la Pléiade, 1951-1999.

GIONO, Jean, *Jean Le Bleu*, Paris, Grasset, 1932; *Le Hussard sur le toit*, Paris, Gallimard, 1951; *Œuvres complètes*, Paris, Gallimard,
Bibliothèque de La Pléiade, 1964; *Le Déserteur et autres récits*, Paris, Gallimard, 1973; *Provence*, Paris, Gallimard, 1993.

HOMÈRE, *L'Odyssée*, translated by Frédéric Mugler, Arles, Actes Sud, 1995.

IZZO, Jean-Claude, *Total Khéops*, Série Noire; *Marseille*, Autrement, 1998.

JOYCE, James, *Ulysse*, translated by A. Morel, Paris, Gallimard, 1989.

KEMAL, Yachar, *La Grotte*, Paris, Gallimard, 1992; *Salih l'émerveillé*, Paris, Gallimard, 1990.

LEIRIS, Michel, *Operratiques*, Paris, POL, 1992.

LEVI, Carlo, *Le Christ s'est arrêté à Eboli*, Paris, Gallimard, 1991.

LUCA, Erri de, *Tu, moi*, Paris, Rivages, 1998; *Rez-de-chaussée*, Paris, Rivages, 1998.

MAALOUF, Amin, *Léon l'Africain*, Paris, Lattès, 1986; *Les Échelles du Levant*, Paris, Grasset, 1996.

MALAPARTE, Curzio, *Kaputt*, Paris, Gallimard, 1969.

MANDIARGUES, André Pieyre de, *La Marge*, Paris, Gallimard, 1967.

MANET, Eduardo, *Viva verdi mare nostrum*, Arles, Actes Sud, 1998.

MANN, Thomas, *La Mort à Venise*, translated by Philippe Jaccottet, Paris, Bibliothèque des arts, 1994.

MAURRAS, Charles, *Le Voyage d'Athènes*, Paris, Flammarion, 1929; *Notre Provence*, avec DAUDET, Léon, Paris, Flammarion, 1933.

MILLER, Henry, *Le Colosse de Maroussi*, translated by Georges Belmont, Paris, Le Livre de poche, 1978.

MORAND, Paul, *Venises*, Paris, Gallimard, 1971; *Bains de mer*, Paris, Le Livre de poche, Biblio, 1992; *Le Voyage*, Paris, Pocket, 1996.

MORAVIA, Alberto, *Le Mépris*, Paris, Flammarion, 1955, Librio, 1999.

ORTESE, Anna Maria, *La Mer ne baigne pas Naples*, Paris, Gallimard, 1993.

ORTLIEB, Gilles, *Gibraltar du Nord*, Cognac, Le temps qu'il fait, 1995.

PAMUK, Ohran, *Le Livre noir*, Paris, Gallimard, 1994.

PELEGRI, Jean, *Les Étés perdus*, Paris, Seuil, 1999; *Ma mère l'Algérie*, Arles, Actes Sud, 1990.

PONGE, Francis, *Pour un Malherbe*, Paris, Gallimard, 1965.

SCHIFANO, Jean-Noël, *Chroniques napolitaines*, Paris, Gallimard, 1984; *La Danse des ardents*, Paris, Gallimard, 1986.

SCIASCIA, Leonardo, *Œuvres*, Paris, Denoël, 1979.

SÉNAC, Jean, *Citoyens de beauté*, Rodez, J. Subervie, 1967; *Avant corps*, Paris, Gallimard, 1968; *Poèmes*, Arles, Actes Sud, 1986; *Pour une terre possible*, Paris, Marsa, 1999.

STYRON, William, *La Proie des flammes*, traduction Maurice-Edgar Coindreau, Paris, Gallimard, 1980.

TANPÏNAR, Ahmet Hamdi, *Cinq villes*, Paris, Publisud, 1995.

TOULET, Paul-Jean, *Œuvres complètes*, Paris, Robert Laffont, Bouquins, 1986.

VALÉRY, Paul, *Œuvres*, Paris, Gallimard, Bibliothèque de la Pléiade, 1975-1977.

VAN GOGH, Vincent, *Lettres à son frère Théo*, Paris, Biblos, 1972.

VIRGILE, *Bucoliques*, translated by Paul Valéry; *Géorgiques*, traduction Jacques Delille, Paris, Gallimard, 1956-1997.

VITTORINI, Elio, *Les Villes du monde*, translated by Michel Arnaud, Paris, Gallimard, 1952; *Conversation en Sicile*, translated by M. Arnaud, Paris, Gallimard, 1990.

Essay

AUDISIO, Gabriel, *Le Sel de la mer*, Paris, Gallimard, 1936.

AUJAC, Germaine, *La Géographie dans le monde antique*, Paris, PUF, 1975.

BARTHES, Roland, *Œuvres complètes, 1942-1980*, Paris, Seuil, 1993-1995.

BAUDOT, François, *Mode du siècle*, Paris, Assouline, 1999; *Alaïa*, Paris, Assouline, 1996.

BENOIST-MECHIN, Jacques, *Frédéric de Hohenstaufen ou le rêve excommunié, 1194–1250*, Paris, Perrin, 1980.

BERQUE, Jacques, *Le Maghreb entre deux guerres*, Paris, Seuil, 1962; *L'Orient second*, Paris, Gallimard, 1970; *Andalousies*, Paris, Sindbad, 1981; *Mémoires des deux rives*, Paris, Seuil, 1989; *L'Islam au défi*, Paris, Gallimard, 1980.

BÉRARD, Victor, *L'Odyssée d'Homère*, Paris, Mellottée, 1927; *Œuvres complètes*, Paris, A.Colin, 1927-1935; *Dans le sillage d'Ulysse*, Paris, A. Colin, 1933; *Introuction à l'Odyssée*, Paris, Les Belles Lettres, 1933; *La Navigation d'Ulysse*, Paris, A. Colin, 1971.

BOUILLON, Jean-Paul, *Maurice Denis*, Genève, Skira, 1993.

BOIME, *Van Gogh, La Nuit étoilée*, Paris, Adam Biro, 1989.

BONNECHERE, Pierre and DE BRUYN, Odile, *L'Art et l'Âme des jardins*, Anvers, Fonds Mercator, 1998.

BOUVIER, Nicolas, *Boissonnas: une dynastie de photographes*, Lausanne, Payot, 1983.

BRAUNSTEIN, Philippe and DELORT, Robert, *Venise, portrait d'une cité*, Paris, Seuil, 1971.

CALLE, Sophie and BAUDRILLARD, Jean, *Suite vénitienne*, Paris, Éd. de l'Étoile, 1983.

CLADEL, Judith, *Aristide Maillol: sa vie, son œuvre, ses idées*, Paris, Grasset, 1937.

CAMPORESI, Piero, *Les Belles Contrées, naissance du paysage italien*, Paris, Le Promeneur, 1995.

CHEBEL, Malek, *L'Imaginaire arabo-musulman*, Paris, PUF, 1993;

La Féminisation du monde, essai sur les Mille et Une Nuits, Paris, Payot, 1996; *Traité du raffinement*, Paris, Payot, 1999.

CORBIN, Alain, *Le Territoire du vide. L'Occident et le désir du rivage*, Paris, Aubier, 1988.

CRESPI, *L'Europe musulmane*, Saint-Léger-Vauban, Zodiaque, 1982.

DUPIN, Jacques, *Miró*, Paris, Flammarion, 1993.

DUPONT, Florence, *Homère et "Dallas"*, Paris, Hachette, 1990; *L'Invention de la littérature*, Paris, Éd. de la Découverte, 1994.

ESCARPIT, *Byron*, Paris, Seghers, 1965.

FELLINI, Ferderico, *Fellini par Fellini*, conversations with G. Greazzini, Paris, Calmann-Levy, 1984.

FORESTIER, J.-C, *Du jardin au paysage urbain*, Paris, Picard, 1994.

GALASSI, Peter, *Corot en Italie*, Paris, Gallimard, 1991.

GODARD, Jean-Luc, *Histoire(s) du cinéma*, Paris, Gallimard, 1998.

GRIMAL, Pierre, *Les Jardins romains*, Paris, PUF, 1969; *L'Art des jardins*, Paris, PUF, 1974.

HUGUES, Robert, *Barcelone, la ville des merveilles*, Paris, Albin Michel, 1992.

JACOB, Christian, *Géographie et Ethnologie en Grèce ancienne*, Paris, A. Colin, 1991; *L'Empire des cartes*, Paris, Albin Michel, 1992.

KANTOROWICZ, Ernst, *L'Empereur Frédéric II*, Paris, Gallimard, Bibliothèque des Histoires, 1987.

KAZAN, Elia, *Kazan par Kazan*, conversations with Michel Ciment, Paris, Ramsay, 1985.

LACOSTE, Yves, *La Géographie, ça sert d'abord à faire la guerre*, Paris, la Découverte, 1985;

La Légende de la Terre, Paris, Flammarion, 1996; *Paysages politiques, Braudel, Gracq, Reclus*, Librairie générale française, 1990.

LACROIX, Christian, *Pêle-Mêle*, Thames & Hudson, 1992.

LIST, Herbert, *Lumière sur la Grèce*, preface by Hugo von Hofmannsthal, Paris, Le Chêne, 1993.

MAALOUF, Amin, *Les Croisades vues par les Arabes*, Paris, Lattès, 1992.

NICOLET, Claude, *L'Inventaire du monde*, Paris, Fayard, 1988.

PERONCEL-HUGOZ, Jean-Pierre, *Le Radeau de Mahomet*, Paris, Flammarion, 1884; *Villes du Sud*, Paris, Balland, 1990.

REMY, Pierre-Jean, *Callas, une vie*, Paris, A.Michel 1997.

ROBERT, Marthe, *L'Ancien et le nouveau: de Don Quichotte à Franz Kafka*, Paris, Grasset, 1963.

SANZIO, Alain, *Visconti cinéaste*, Paris, Persona, 1984.

SERRES, Michel, *Atlas*, Paris, Le Grand Livre du mois, 1994.

STASSINOPOULOS, Arianna, *Maria Callas par-delà sa légende*, Paris, Fayard, 1981.

TERRASSE, Antoine, *Bonnard*, Paris, Gallimard, 1988.

THARAUD, Jérôme, *La Fête arabe*, La Tour-d'Aigues, Éd. de l'Aube, 1997.

TRYSTAM, Florence, *Terre! Terre!*, Paris, Jean-Claude Lattès, 1994.

URBAIN, Jean-Didier, *L'Idiot du voyage, Histoires de touristes*, Paris, Payot et Rivages, 1993;

Sur la plage, Paris, Payot, 1994.

VOGT-GOKNIL, Ulya, *Mosquées*, Paris, Le Chêne, 1975.

Photographic credits

Cover: © Musée des Beaux-Arts de Berne—**p. 4-5:** © Collections of Centre Georges Pompidou, musée national d'Art moderne, Paris—
p. 6: New York, Metropolitan Museum of Art. © Photo: George Hoyningen-Huene/Fiona Cowan—**p. 9:** © Erich Lessing/AKG Paris/Adagp, Paris 2000—**p. 11:** London, Tate Gallery. © AKG Paris/Adagp, Paris 2000—**p. 13:** © Paris, cliché Bibliothèque nationale de France—**p. 15:** © Bodleian Library, Oxford, U.K. — **p. 17:** Private Collection. © Estate of H. Matisse/Giraudon—**p. 20:** © Fondation Dinah Vierny – musée Maillol, Paris/Adagp, Paris 2000—**p. 22-23:** The Barnes Foundation, Merion, Pennsylvania. © Succession H. Matisse/AKG Paris—**p. 25:** Saint-Petersburg, Ermitage Museum. © Catalogue raisonné Maurice Denis/Adagp, Paris 2000—**p. 27:** Paris, Picasso Museum. © RMN/J.G. Berizzi/Estate of Picasso 2000—
p. 28-29: © Adagp, Paris 2000—**p. 31:** Düsseldorf, Kunstmuseum. © Kunstmuseum Düsseldorf im Ehrenhof/Dauerleihgabe der Staatlichen Kunstakademie—**p. 32:** New York, Museum of Modern Art. © AKG Paris—**p. 33:** Paris, musée d'Orsay. © Photo: RMN—**p. 34-35:** Mairie de Montreuil, Hôtel de Ville. © Erich Lessing/AKG Paris/Adagp, Paris 2000—**p. 38:** Düsseldorf, Kunstmuseum. © AKG Paris—**p. 39:** © Zefa-Streichan/HOA-QUI—
p. 40-41: Paris, Private Collection. © Estate of Picasso 2000/Giraudon—**p. 45:** Paris, musée d'Orsay. © Photo: C. Jean/RMN—**p. 47:** © Archives Borel-Boissonnas—**p. 48-49:** © Photo: George Hoyningen-Huene/Fiona Cowan—**p. 51:** © Photo: Karl Lagerfeld/Steidl—**p. 53:** © Photo: Herbert List/Magnum—**p. 55:** © Collection *Les Cahiers du cinéma*—**p. 56-57:** Photos from the film *Contempt*, with courtesy of Jean-Luc Godard—
p. 58: © AKG Paris—**p. 59:** © D.R./Collection *Les Cahiers du cinéma*—**p. 61:** © Collection *Les Cahiers du cinéma*—**p. 63:** © Gilles Mermet/AKG Paris—**p. 64:** © AKG Paris—**p. 65-66:** © Photo: Hans Silvester/Rapho—**p. 69:** London, British Museum. Collection Canino. © Erich Lessing/AKG Paris—**p. 71:** Bonn, Rheinisches Landesmuseum. © Erich Lessing/AKG Paris—**p. 72:** Versailles et Trianon. © RMN/D. Arnaudet/G.B.—
p. 73: Paris, Bibliothèque nationale de France. © Lauros/Giraudon—**p. 75:** Paris, Bibliothèque nationale de France. © AKG Paris—
p. 77: © Photo: Sam Levin/ministère de la Culture, France—**p. 78:** Private Collection. © Photothèque René Magritte/Giraudon/Adagp, Paris 2000—
p. 80-81 *(from left to right)* : © Artephot/R. Perrin. © Michael Woolworth Publications. Paris, musée du Louvre. © AKG Paris—**p. 83 :** Munich, Neue Pinakothek. © AKG Paris—**p. 84:** © Photo: Bruce Davidson/Magnum—**p. 85:** © Photo: Léo Pelissier/Rapho—**p. 87:** Private Collection. © AKG Paris—
p. 88-89: Paris, musée du Louvre. © RMN/H. Lewandowski—**p. 92-93:** © Photo: Isabel Munoz/ Agence Vu—**p. 95:** © AKG Paris—
p. 96-97: Marseille, musée des Beaux-Arts. © Giraudon—**p. 98:** Paris, musée du Louvre, D.A.G. © J.-G. Berizzi/RMN — **p. 99:** Paris, musée du Louvre. © Giraudon—**p. 101:** © N. D./Viollet—**p. 103:** Madrid, Photographic Archives of the Senado. © Artephot/Oronoz—**p. 104-105:** © Photo: Anderson-Viollet—**p. 106:** © Courtesy Galerie Tony Shafrazi, New York—**p. 107:** Sevilla, Archeological Museum. © Artephot/Nimattallah—
p. 111: © Estate of H. Matisse—**p. 112:** Paris, musée du Louvre. © Lauros/Giraudon—**p. 113:** © Éditions Oum—**p. 114-115:** Toulouse, musée des Augustins. © AKG Paris—**p. 117:** Washington, National Gallery. © Artephot/Oronoz—**p. 118-119:** © Photo: Tony Vaccaro/AKG Paris—
p. 120 *(from left to right):* Collection Count Raczynski. Poznan, National Museum. © AKG Paris. © Photo: Guy Le Guerrec/Magnum—
p. 121: © Laziz Hamani/Éditions Assouline—**p. 122:** Paris, musée d'Orsay. © AKG Paris/Adagp, Paris 2000—**p. 123:** © Collection Viollet—
p. 125: © Photo: Georges Viollon/Rapho—**p. 126:** © Photo: Ferdinando Scianna/Magnum—**p. 127:** Athènes, musée national d'Archéologie. © John Hios/AKG Paris—**p. 128:** © Photo: Agnès Bonnot/Agence Vu—**p. 129:** © Photo: Jean Gaumy/Magnum—**p. 131:** © Archives SBM—
p. 132: © Collection Viollet—**p. 133:** © Photo: Denis Dailleux/Agence Vu—**p. 134-135:** Private Collection of Mariane and Pierre Nahon. Château Notre-Dame-des-Fleurs, Vence. © Adagp, Paris 2000—**p. 137:** Private Collection. © Adagp, Paris 2000—**p. 139:** © Photo: Erio Piccagliani/Archivio Fotografico Teatro alla Scala—**p. 140:** © KIPA—**p. 141:** © Photo: Herbert List/Magnum—**p. 143:** © Cliché Bibliothèque nationale de France, Paris—**p. 144-145:** © Photo: Eric Franceschi/Agence Vu—**p. 146-147:** © AKG Paris—**p. 150:** © Laziz Hamani/Éditions Assouline—
p. 151: Los Angeles, Los Angeles County Museum of Art, Estate of Hans G. M. de Schulthess. © 2000, Museum Associates, Los Angeles County Museum of Art/Adagp, Paris 2000—**p. 152:** © Photo: L. L. Roger-Viollet. Collection Viollet—**p. 155:** © Photo: Woitek Buss/HOA-QUI—**p. 156:** Urbino, Galleria Nazionale delle Marche. © S. Dominige – M. Rabatti/AKG Paris—**p. 157:** © Lauros/Giraudon/Adagp, Paris 2000—**p. 158-159:** © Photo: Mario de Biasi—**p. 161:** Otterlo, Rijksmuseum Kröller-Müller. © Erich Lessing/AKG Paris—**p. 162:** © Photo: Jean Marc Tingaud—
p. 163 et 167: © Éditions Oum—**p. 168:** © Photo: Jean Marc Tingaud—**p. 169:** Moscou, Pouchkine Museum. © Estate of H. Matisse/AKG Paris—
p. 170 : Paris, Petit-Palais. © Lauros/Giraudon—**p. 173:** © Jean Marc Tingaud—**p. 174:** © Zefa-Damm/HOA-QUI—**p. 175:** © Éditions Assouline—
p. 177: © Photo: Anne Rearick/Agence Vu—**p. 178:** Paris, musée du Louvre. © Laziz Hamani/Éditions Assouline—**p. 179:** © Photo: Laziz Hamani/Éditions Assouline—**p. 183:** © AKG Paris—**p. 184:** Paris, musée d'Orsay. Prêt du groupe GAN. © Erich Lessing/AKG Paris—**p. 185:** © Photo: Philippe Saharoff—**p. 186:** © Éditions Assouline—**p. 187:** University of Illinois Archives—**p. 188:** Rome, Museo Nazionale Romano delle Terme. © AKG Paris—**p. 191:** © Éditions Assouline—**p. 192-193:** © Laziz Hamani/Éditions Assouline—**p. 195:** © Photo: Olivier Wogensky—**p. 197:** © Photo: Laziz Hamani/Éditions Assouline—**p. 198-199:** Photo: Jacques-Henri Lartigue. © Ministère de la Culture, France/A.A.J.H.L. — **p. 200:** Collection Vincent Pinel. © Photo: Raymond Cauchetier—**p. 201:** © Éditions Assouline—**p. 202-203:** Paris, Collections of Centre Georges Pompidou/musée national d'Art moderne. © Estate of Miró/Adagp, Paris 2000—**p. 205:** © Photo: Pierre Olivier Deschamps/Agence Vu—**p. 206:** © Éditions Oum—
p. 208: Saint-Petersburg, Ermitage Museum. Collection S.I. Schtschukin. © Estate of H. Matisse/AKG Paris—**p. 209:** Paris, Archives Larousse. © Archives Larousse/Giraudon—**p. 213:** © Photo: David Douglas Duncan—**p. 214:** © Photo: Laziz Hamani/Éditions Assouline—
p. 215: © Photo: Jean Marie del Moral—**p. 217:** © Photo: M. Vanden Eeckhoudt/Rapho—**p. 218:** © Photo: David Dare Parker/ Agence Vu—
p. 219: © Éditions Assouline—**p. 220** *(from left to right)* : © KIPA. © Photo: F. Le Diascorn/Agence Vu—**p. 221:** © Collection *Les Cahiers du cinéma*—
p. 222: © Private Collection – Roux Family—**p. 223:** Paris, Collections of Centre Georges Pompidou/musée national d'Art moderne.
© Estate of H. Matisse—**p. 225:** Paris, Picasso Museum/ Archives Picasso. © Estate of Picasso 2000—**p. 227:** © Photo: Keiichi Tahara/Adagp, Paris 2000—**p. 228:** © Photo: Jean Marie del Moral—**p. 232:** © Photo: Robert Descharnes/Descharnes & Descharnes—
p. 233: © Photo: Michel Georges-Michel/Estate of H. Matisse.

Acknowledgments

The publisher wishes to thank:
Brigitte Bardot, Jean Charles Blais, Margaret Burnham, Raymond Cauchetier, Robert and Olivier Descharnes, David Douglas Duncan, Jean-Luc Godard, Laziz Hamani, Joyce de R., Karl Lagerfeld, Gina Lollobrigida, Joan Punyet Miró, Jean-Marie del Moral, Marianne and Pierre Nahon, Éric Pfrunder, Philippe Saharoff, Keiichi Tahara, Jean Marc Tingaud, Olivier Wogensky, Michael Woolworth ; as well as AKG Photo (Fabienne, Hervé and Ülrike), Artephot (Pascale), Association des amis de Jacques-Henri Lartigue (François-Xavier Lorrain), musée des Beaux-Arts de Berne (Regula Zbinden), Bibliothèque nationale de France, Bodleian Library in Oxford, Gad and Cléo Borel of Archives Borel-Boissonnas, photothèque des *Cahiers du cinéma* (Benoît), Fiona Cowan (Hamiltons Photographers Limited), musée départemental Maurice Denis, museum of Fine Arts in Düsseldorf (Anne-Marie Katins), Véronique Garrigues (Adagp), Giraudon (Muriel), Wanda de Guébriant (Estate of H. Matisse), HOA-QUI (Elizabeth), Kipa, The Los Angeles County Museum of Art (Cheryle Robertson), Magnum Photo (Marie-Christine Biebuyck), Éditions Oum (Mohamed Sijelmassi), Patrimoine photographique (Anne-Catherine), the Estate of Picabia, the Picasso Administration, Photothèque du Centre Georges Pompidou (Mrs. Charton), Rapho (Kathy), Photographic Agency of RMN (Frédérique Kartouby), the Archives of the Scala (Elena Fumagalli), the Tony Shafrazy Gallery in New York, Fondation Dinah Vierny-musée Maillol, Roger-Viollet and Agence Vu (Malika).